No More
SECRETS
No More
LIES

No More
SECRETS
No More
LIES

A Handbook
to Starseed Awakening

PATRICIA CORI

North Atlantic Books
Berkeley, California

Published by
North Atlantic Books
P.O. Box 12327
Berkeley, California 94712

Cover photograph courtesy of the European Southern Observatory
Cover and book design by Brad Greene

Printed in the United States of America

No More Secrets, No More Lies: A Handbook to Starseed Awakening is sponsored by the Society for the Study of Native Arts and Sciences, a nonprofit educational corporation whose goals are to develop an educational and cross-cultural perspective linking various scientific, social, and artistic fields; to nurture a holistic view of arts, sciences, humanities, and healing; and to publish and distribute literature on the relationship of mind, body, and nature.

North Atlantic Books' publications are available through most bookstores. For further information, call 800-733-3000 or visit our Web site at www.northatlanticbooks.com.

Library of Congress Cataloging-in-Publication Data

Cori, Patricia.
    No more secrets, no more lies : a handbook to starseed awakening / Patricia Cori.
        p. cm.
    Summary: "Uncovers how ancient prophecies are playing out in the political and geophysical events of contemporary life on Earth and calls on humanity to shine the light of truth on its darkest fears, thus preparing the way for further human and celestial evolution"—Provided by publisher.
    ISBN-13: 978-1-55643-738-0
    ISBN-10: 1-55643-738-2
    1. Prophecies (Occultism) 2. Civilization, Modern—21st century—Forecasting. I. Title.
    BF1791.C596 2008
    299'.93—dc22
                                                                                    2007041244
                                                                                    CIP

3 4 5 6 7 8 9 10 UNITED 14 13 12 11 10 09

Table of Contents

Part I
Light upon Darkness

1

Let There Be
No More Secrets

As you delve ever deeper into the true origins of your race, you are realizing that the establishment's tales of human history are far too limiting and that they are filled with deception, glaring omissions, and countless errors. You try to put the real picture together, attempting to decipher the tattered pages of ancient texts and the maps of your great ancestors, but so little remains in the written record—a mere whisper on the winds of ages.

The loss of your most important historical records and the incredible esoteric knowledge contained within them is not only due to the natural processes of Earth's evolution and the illusive passing of "time." What little survived of the antediluvian record was systematically destroyed by soldiers and the masked crusaders, who have been serving the Power since so long ago that your contemporary cultures cannot imagine such expanses of time ... much less remember them.

Consider, too, that countless volumes of the most significant material (those which speak in detail of the true origins of your race and of the extraterrestrial forces that have influenced your development) were sequestered by the Authority and its secret societies, to be hoarded in the vaults of their private collections, far from the eyes of the common people. These have been quietly passed down over generations—from one covert hand to another—always far from the public's line of vision.

Many of the great works of your ancestors are locked away to this very day ... for the Power still believes that knowledge of Earth's true history is theirs to deny you—just as they have managed, throughout your existence, to conceal the truth of their conspiracy to control and suppress the human race, while raping Planet Earth of its riches.

They are mistaken.

The true story of your roots—your incredible journey—is being slowly retrieved from the keys that have been "buried" by the ancients, just as it is being beamed to you upon the waves of consciousness coming into Earth's fields at this point in your ascension process and brought to full awareness from your subconscious recall (where the soul's multidimensional experience is reflected back to you as "memory"). This you are discovering in these hours of change and renewal ... and much more will become available in the days that lie just ahead of you.

The Wisdom will be secret no more.

Soon to be opened is the Atlantean Hall of Records—inextricably linked to the Great Sphinx at Giza. In ways that have somehow escaped your probing curiosity, **it is the very Sphinx itself.** Fortunately, the Atlantean codex remains intact, for the establishment archeological community is focused upon gold-filled chambers filled with historical records and artifacts, but there are far greater treasures buried there, in the cool sands that lie deep below the mysterious feline effigy.

The Hall contains access codes to the multidimensional cosmic library. These were deposited by Priests of the White Brotherhood, who descended from the safety of the highlands and migrated to the Nile River Valley of Egypt when the waters finally receded. They were to encode the Wisdom there, to be guarded for generations by their direct descendents—the first Pharaohs. The Hall of Records was left as a legacy to humankind, entrusted for safe-keeping to the enigmatic lioness, until that point in time when you would be ready to enter the Atlantean chamber—a sacred space—and bring forward the codex, opening a window upon the no-time of human evolution.

That is about to take place ... in your lifetimes, as you decreed it.

More is buried in the tales and legends of select indigenous peoples, those Keepers of the Records who have managed to retain their heritage, the "connection," and the memory. As you begin to recognize the Keepers for who they really are, they, in turn, are cautiously dipping into the treasure chests of the past to bring to the world the pearls of ancestral knowledge. More will be coming forward as you approach the closing of the Mayan Calendar, which will have initiated December 21, 2012.

The Keepers of the Crystals will hold open the portals; Keepers of Time will help you move through them. This has been known to the Maya since their Elders first peered through the crystal skulls and realized that Earth, reborn fourfold, would reach the *Fifth Sun* at the end of 2012 AD and enter its final phase of ascension from the universe of matter into the fourth dimension—where the illusion of time no longer exists.

More of you are learning to read the Akashic Record, where all is foreseen ... all is remembered. Those with the gift of sight and a spiritual orientation understand that what you term "past" and "future" are simply aspects of the forever, existing eternally in the no-time of all Creation. So it is that, although we make constant allusion to linear time (for that is a point of reference in your existing terminology), we invite you to remain acutely aware of its illusory nature. Throughout our teachings, we ask you to consider how all events occur simultaneously, constantly, intertwined in the great cosmic dance of consciousness, unfolding and slowly ascending the spiral of spiritual return.

We, Speakers of the Sirian High Council, are dedicated to helping you unravel the story of your evolution—back from the days of your seeding and forward, towards the very near moment of your passing from the third dimension. We wish to help you live in the "now" of this most magnificent moment of your journey, at peace with your planet, your neighbors, and yourselves.

In *The Cosmos of Soul,* we have shown you the process of your Solar Deity's ascension and projected you out onto the fourth dimension, which you are soon to know in light body. Our last effort, *Atlantis Rising,* was dedicated to facilitating the release of some of your most difficult memories of Atlantis, while empowering you with the knowledge that you need now . . . if you are to free yourselves from the new alchemists of power and move forward in the light of your growing awareness.

Indeed, in viewing the events occurring upon your planet, we discern that the awakening amongst you are coming out of hiding, speaking your truth as never before. Your throats are open, and you are communicating with great clarity and focus, beaming Gaia's cobalt blue ray through all the Cosmos.

You are preparing now to refute the authority and take charge of your personal realities, defying the censure that is being placed over the voice of your growing dissidence. Never forget that your individual experiences of growth and enlightenment are meant to be shared with the greater community if they are to affect the greater whole, whereby all of humanity moves into positive mind space and the necessary changes—those that are already becoming manifest at determined points of the globe—can begin to sweep the entire planet.

This is the time of global awakening.

Let there be no more secrets ... no more lies.

To assist you in this most important phase of your reveille, we have called upon the channel to bring through this third missive, knowing that it is a most controversial collection of teachings. Here we are determined to help you pull out all the stops and get "Sirius" about what is going on around you. This, the third book of the trilogy, is dedicated to facilitating your understanding of the events that have led to your disempowerment, while revealing the most pressing concerns surrounding the great conspiracy that, for millennia, has deterred and suppressed the human race. It is intended as a guide to your liberation from the designs of the dark warriors and designed to serve as a manual for clearing your minds of the debris that has settled as "conviction" in your belief systems.

It is a handbook to starseed awakening.

For far too long, humankind has been denied the truth regarding the covert management of your planet, but that is coming to an end in your lifetimes. Observe, and you cannot but see the web of deceit and lies unraveling: the towers of power are collapsing all around you.

The nature of your experience at this time on Planet Earth is one of awakening to all that exists, reaching for the beyond and the within of all things—where Truth, so precious and so pure, can no longer elude you.

The Light Forces of the Universe have gathered to assist in this process, for you have called out and we are here. We, the Sirians, are right here beside you, so close you cannot imagine, existing in a parallel reality that is just as much your experience as it is our own ... and we have traveled your road, where the vapors of illusion veil the pathway.

We understand how difficult it can be to find the way home. We know how arduous is the initiation that you are facing as the new dawn beckons you to rise ... and to sleep no more.

We have come to you with the keys to your inner doorways, to help you move past all barriers and claim, for all of humanity, the knowledge buried in the secret covenants—knowledge that will release you from the holds of the puppeteers who are pulling to the snapping point the strings of the human race.

Although you may still be unclear about your individual assignments, know that you have chosen to take a significant role in the unfolding "future" of your species and the living beings of Gaia.

Your minds are open, filled with wonder... and yet you have very clear ideas about the human condition. Despite appearances, you trust that all that which is occurring now must, by nature of the All That Is, be an expression of the Divine Plan, yet you see the direction in which your contemporary societies are headed. You know that you are the New Aquarians and that, together with the children, you have come in to help guide the course of humanity as you approach the new frontier.

Yours will be the task of storming the imposed boundaries and releasing the knowledge you have been actively acquiring for the good of all the living beings of your world and of the universe that surrounds and penetrates you.

This, the third collection of transmissions through our vehicle, Trydjya, is a decidedly daring endeavor. It is dedicated to revealing the secrets that may still have evaded your discovery, while bringing into focus the events unfolding right in front of your eyes—eyes that all too often do not see what lies unmistakably in plain view or that simply refuse to look. It is a challenge to the dogma of religion and government, while it is a revealer of the truths that you carry within every cell, every micro-measure of your being. It serves as a "handbook" to the reactivation of dormant intelligence codes within you and as a guide to the free-will seekers of universal truth and cosmic order.

We intend to expose, for once and forever, the lies that are being fed to the global earth society, while leading you to the "secret" libraries of stored knowledge that have been closed from the time of your seeding—the etheric DNA that is beginning to crystallize and rebundle within you. You will be guided to stare right into the storm, raising your swords to the dragon, and to charge straight ahead into the dark night of your fear—leading those who have yet to find the way to the Wisdom and the Light.

You will be victorious. You, who seek out our message, are the bold new warriors—let there be no question of that. You dare to think for yourselves, to challenge the status quo, and to demand answers in a world where the pieces no longer seem to fit. The establishment's story of your past and its projections of your future do not do justice to the human race, and so we anticipate your questions. We are here to provide what answers we can in the light of your quest.

We are here for you ... and for the children.

We are not so presumptuous to imply that we understand all the mysteries underlying the manifestations of Supreme Consciousness, for we are as you ... children of the heavens. Like you, we are curious travelers upon the evolutionary spiral, learning more at every turn—seeking illumination and the Return. Yet, we believe that it is our responsibility, as lightworkers of these realms, to serve and assist you, by gifting you with whatever knowledge we can bring through for you, while guiding you inward to activate that place of "knowing" ... the lighthouse of the soul.

So it is that we have undertaken the preparation of this latest manuscript, in which we trust you will uncover answers to some of those questions that have haunted and disturbed you at the conscious and subconscious levels—questions that can no longer go unanswered or be pushed into the dark corners of your distracted indifference or fearful minds.

You may surely find, in the text of these pages, information that accomplishes that task—information you are now prepared to hear. These, the imprinted words that have come through the channel, we ask you to consider as the "crystallization" of our conscious emanations ... but there is more.

Our channel's increasing ability to hold resonance at higher frequencies has facilitated the appearance and participation of luminary eight-dimensional beings for these specific transmissions, which complete the Trilogy—*The Sirian Revelations.* She has prepared for this assignment, and yet theirs is a frequency of such vibrational intensity that they cannot yet link with her directly.

Serving as filters for these extraordinary emissions, we feel the light waves moving through us, for we, too, receive attunement in the process. These are gifts of Spirit, and we are forever grateful to you for the opportunities you create throughout the Universe—radiating your love across the Gossamer Web of Light. We are grateful and honored to be given the opportunity to bathe in such brilliance, while serving as a sort of cosmic transducer of the awesome light waves that are coming in at this time, moving through us expressly **for you.**

We have been instructed that these Ascension Teams have joined us to enhance the material via light-encrypted supraliminal codes, to help move you through your residual emotions. It is their intention to help heal the fragments of your personae, as you shine the bright light of knowledge directly into your lower chakras and then bring the trauma of trapped memories up into full consciousness, to be cleansed and forgiven. There will be stimulation of the pineal gland and great expansion in the heart center—you have this to look forward to.

Most of this will occur at a level of awareness that is beyond words, without instruction or guidance. It will be effortless. The process of adjustment and energy shifting, as we have been made to understand it, will be facilitated throughout the text by the interweaving of high-intensity vibrational frequencies, which will be perceived and integrated in your auric fields as light moving through the energy byways of your beings and into the pineal gland—the lighthouse of your souls.

For many, this will be experienced as subtle shifting in your mental, emotional, and physical bodies, while for others it may manifest as powerful emotional reactions or physical release. Dream states may be enhanced, so that you may have conscious recollection of your astral journeys in the sleeping hours, and many of you will find your perception of the spirit world is becoming more "tangible." You may exalt in the experience of liberating, joyful emotions or find you are suddenly confronted with pent-up anger or deep resentment, as those blocked emotions move through you and away.

This process involves releasing those frozen energies that are still holding you in fear. You may want to throw down this book altogether, refusing to open the floodgates. That, Dear Ones, is your choice to make and we invite you to follow your hearts.

We ask you to consider, however, that the release of negative thought forms and blocked energies can be a difficult process, but that it is a fundamental aspect of light-body awakening. If you should feel compelled to "blame" the material for any emotional discomfort that may arise, know that the message, of itself, is not the cause. You may want to consider, instead, how the upset lies in the fear and parallel emotions that you are inevitably pushing yourselves to confront (for once and forever) as your planet prepares for the final phases of ascension and you mutate from the chrysalis to take wing.

For those of you still stuck in survival and others who have not yet begun the work of clearing, we are committed to jump-starting that process here. We believe you made that free-will decision when you reached for this book and first opened its cover.

You, who have long ago opened the way, will achieve further clarity of that which you already know—your truth—while the extraordinary waves of light moving through you will facilitate your attunement and further accelerate the awakening.

We invite you all to call upon your Spirit Guides to validate that this process is for your highest purpose. Know that your guides are always there for you and that they serve as the sentinels of your souls. We, too, call upon guidance as a screening process of our interdimensional encounters. This is a practice that should become (if it is not already) so natural to you that you needn't even think about it.

We ask you to trust and to recognize our intention and that of the Light Ones of many dimensions. Allow yourselves to feel and to respond to our message, never suppressing the surfacing of buried emotions. If you are going to serve as awakeners—true spirit warriors—you must first resolve your survival issues, silencing those gnawing fears in order to release from your inertia and swing into the action zone. You can walk in the light of knowledge, free of the torments that bind you, once you let go of fear. You will then move through the Earth Changes unscathed, knowing where you are headed and what awaits you once you arrive.

Therefore, do not give up on us when the first waves begin to rush through you, for it is our intention to move you, and it is your intention to be moved.

And you will.

You chose this material for a reason.

You are well on your way, cleared for take-off.

⁘

So let us fly the skies of your imagination, exploring the periphery of visions that may have escaped you until now, because there is so much you want to know about us and about yourselves, about the material realm and the multidimensional universe, about the darkness and the light.

Although you thoroughly enjoy savoring the idea that yours is the "information generation"—inventor of vast telecommunications systems that have put your electronic fingers on the pulse of the entire globe even as they reach out into space—you remain, paradoxically, one of the most isolated species in existence. The mass population, trained to look no further, still knows nothing of the intelligent universe. This is a wonder to countless civilizations populating the universe of matter . . . and it is even more bewildering to those who constantly fill your night skies with their mechanical flying ships and holographic projections.

There is untold commerce and exchange amongst alien nations, federations of interplanetary cooperation, travel, cultural exchange, and genetic blending. The material universe is bursting with life—filled with the incredible—and, as on Earth, the struggle between the dark and light forces exists, in varying degrees, at every juncture. That duality is a constant of existence, which refines its contrastive nature as we ascend the spiral, reaching for full illumination, where polarity resolves and all individual units of consciousness eventually merge back into Source.

Despite all the signs and communications that come through

for you—despite the mother ships and sightings and transmissions such as ours—most of the human race still holds tightly to the belief that Earth is the true center of the Universe and that yours is the only planet hospitable for life . . . in any form whatsoever. Even though growing numbers of you are awakening to a cosmic perception of the conscious Universe, an overwhelming majority still refuses to believe just how small a speck Earth is in the body of the Cosmos or that you are as minute to the universe of the living as a grain of sand is to the shore.

We have difficulty imagining how you can live with such a sense of loneliness, yet it helps us comprehend your spiritual dilemma. It helps us understand how you have for so long been dominated, controlled, and suppressed as a people. But we have good news for the human race. We are telling you, as are those who are connecting to you through other superb channels or reaching you directly in the dreamtime, that **the time of your isolation is over.**

In spite of the hostile messages the governors of your species send out across the waves, your brothers and sisters of the material universe are moving ever closer, seeking ways to approach without being destroyed or creating mass panic amongst you. That is no easy task, for the Secret Government still does not believe you are ready—nor are they prepared to release you. And so, the message being sent into the Cosmos by the militia that rules your planet is less than inviting, and their alien allies of the dark persuasion are just as forbidding.

Let us paint a picture for you, through which you can see yourselves, for just an instant, as some members of your greater galactic family look upon you and your planet from afar.

Besides the alien civilizations that have already connected with Earth or that are capable of studying you in detail, there are yet other remote worlds that have attuned, in varying degrees, to your realm.

Many are the extraterrestrial beings who, in studying Gaia's atmospheric conditions, electromagnetic emissions, and violent eruptions, surmise that Earth is a discordant, violent planet, clearly inhabited by some form of intelligent life.

Here, it seems, is a technologically advancing civilization, responsible for causing highly disruptive electromagnetic frequencies to course through the planetary body and out into deep space—a civilization with an apparent disregard for the sanctity of space and what appears to be a total lack of awareness of the consequences of its actions.

Observers of your planet find it is encased in a clutter of satellite devices, most of which are bouncing electromagnetic waves of varying degree back and forth from the surface, rather than serving as humanity's voice out into space. Many are armed weapons systems, and these, too, are pointing down at you. This is understood to serve as some primitive kind of control network—the paranoid behavior of an unevolved governing body, which (whatever the intended purpose) appears to be holding the planet hostage while discouraging interplanetary exchange. That, of itself, is a most revealing insight into the living conditions there.

Numerous alien scientific-research teams have intercepted an unnatural electromagnetic grid encircling the planet—an indication that some form of aggressive intervention has occurred during its evolution. Studies conducted by their astronomers have identified holes in this matrix, particularly (but not limited to) the polar regions and parts of the equatorial belt . . . and in those regions of extreme thermonuclear radiation. Diverse alien scientific commissions studying Earth have deduced that this energy grid is disintegrating and that such peculiar satellite mechanisms may be an attempt to reweave an ancient girdle of controlling frequencies around the surface.

Judging from the perennial explosion of nuclear weapons that have been recorded there, the planet is believed to be inhabited by warring, violent beings, who (given what most of the intelligent universe understands about radiation) may be nearing the point of extinction. And it is seen as a destructive population, one that is burning the green belts that supply its oxygen, ripping apart its atmosphere, and filling the blue waters—the source of all life there—with the blackness of its own unprocessed waste.

And we ask you: do you really wonder why beings from other worlds are so terribly hesitant to show themselves to you?

There are others, those whose mother ships are currently journeying just aside of Earth's auric body. The prototype has been shown to you through the time traveler, Gene Roddenberry, whose science-fiction accounts of the activities of the Galactic Federation were anything but fictional.

Theirs is a firsthand awareness of the situation on Planet Earth, for they have been moving through your quadrant of space for some time now, observing the events leading up to your Sun's ascension from the third dimension. They are close enough to observe and study you, and they see beyond the smoke and static that permeates the space around you. They see the crisis in which you find yourselves, just as they see the greatness of humankind—

the beauty beneath the clouds. And, although universal law does not allow their direct intervention, they do monitor the Secret Government and the alien nations with which they are in strict collaboration.

They are aware of your struggle.

Of the multidimensional Universe, where conscious beings from universes parallel to yours and other dimensions are operating alongside and within you, there is a totally different perspective of life and the drama that plays out in the material realms. As you ascend out of material reality, you, too, will recognize the physical reality as a hologram of thought projections crystallized in the no-time, one which serves as a training ground for the soul.

While one is holding this frequency, the illusion of physical reality is so very convincing—and well you know. But from our perspective, it is like watching a movie whose characters seem very real and whose portrayal evokes mental, emotional, and even physical responses ... yet all the while, the viewer knows that it is mere invention. (S)he knows that it is the creative projection of an inspired mind who envisioned the story, selected the cast, wrote the script, and directed the players to make the illusion appear so very real that it is capable of evoking the primordial response.

These are mysteries that you are unraveling now, as you move beyond the viewing screens of your material experience—the illusions of your physical realm—and begin to take flight.

Children of Gaia, we are committed to facilitating this process

... providing what guidance we can in the face of your Great Initiation.

Let us serve as way-stations of incredible radiance and the love of beings who are working through us, refracting their brilliant golden white light through these words (crystals of Sirian consciousness) and into your bodies, minds, and souls.

The tempest is almost behind you now, and just ahead, just over the hill, the new dawn of your infinite existence is breaking on a most breathtaking horizon.

The light that shines there, Dear Ones, you have only just begun to imagine.

2

The Seeding of *Homo Sapiens*

We wish to take you on a vision quest to a point on the time-space continuum that we can best define as having occurred, in your terms of linear time, more than one hundred thousand years ago. It marks a most significant point in the unfolding events of your galactic quadrant, when interference from highly destructive energies led the Forces of Light from many dimensions to become directly involved, justified by its serving as an act of "consequence," rather than one of intervention.

Calls for help from the higher realms raced from the universe of matter through the light strings of the Cosmos, and we simply could not ignore them—although we knew better than to intervene directly in the unfolding events of those civilizations.

As the call pealed like church bells across the heavens, Light Forces from the higher dimensions, Angelic Beings, and the Celestial Deities joined together to help heal the space, radiating waves of love and light to the living of the physical realm and willing that the balance be restored. Many conscious beings of the fifth and sixth dimensions retrograded back into matter, giving birth to a new wave of lightworkers, who would help restore the balance of darkness and light in the 3D theater. Slowly, the energies shifted, and the pendulum began to swing back to center.

There, where the light shone into the blackness, was a renaissance of Spirit, and the Gossamer Web of Light scintillated with the radiance. Still, the density of matter seemed to pull at the collective soul, and it was not long thereafter that the lower vibrations once again threw your realm into violent discord.

That struggle continues eternally, for such is the nature of the Universe. The denser the realm, the greater the polarity that pulls and pushes consciousness from its crystalline expressions of cosmometric perfection into such shattered manifestations of discord and disruption as you are currently experiencing at so many levels of your earthly existence. In the duality of the universe of matter, this is a necessary process, and we remind you that the dissolution of matter is every bit as beautiful as its creation, for both aspects are interdependent upon each other.

As beings, planets, stars, and entire galaxies ascend the spiral of evolution, others are newly born into matter, and with these "newborns" the process begins anew. This is what holds the Universe in balance.

It is the nature of all existence.

Despite the waves of Light Ones who had retrograded back into physical reality, our Elders realized that the balance was completely upset in your universe, that the light was dimming, and that there were far too few incarnate lightworkers to dramatically alter the vibrational pattern that was forming in three-dimensional space and reestablish the balance. It appeared that, without divine assistance, the realm you know as the universe would sink into abysmal darkness—and finally reach extinction.

A Council was formed of Angel Warriors, Andromedans, Ascended Masters, luminaries from the seventh, eighth, and ninth dimensions, Sirian Elders, and Pleiadian Light Emissaries to determine the most effective way to serve the light in those realms. They were circumspect, for they knew that, by intervening, they would be altering the karma of entire civilizations, forever tethered in the dynamics of material space. Together, they gave birth to the idea of seeding a super race of light beings who would go on to serve as monitors of the material universe— the New Sentinels of Light.

That, Dear Ones, was **your** destiny.

A call went out across the Gossamer Web, and word soon spread throughout the Universe that such an experiment—the birthing of a race of light-bodied physical beings capable of anchoring the higher frequencies—was in the planning stages. The daring design born from their union was shared with light-workers of those three-dimensional worlds in distress and the Light Ones of higher dimensions. Stepping ever-so-lightly over the boundary lines of universal law, the Council "connected" with leaders of many remote civilizations ... that they might join in. The replies were overwhelmingly (but not **entirely**) in favor of *The Starseed Project*.

The first consideration was the selection of a hospitable planet that could provide the most favorable conditions in which to incubate a master species of light-bodied physical beings. It had to be one that could remain isolated long enough for the race to be safely germinated, to crystallize and find the perfect environment in which to proliferate. Yet, the host planet would have to be accessible to the galactic community of alien worlds, which would eventually participate in its development. It had to be one that offered ideal atmospheric and biological environments, but which had not yet developed an advancing intelligent species, for that would surely have altered the outcome ... just as the experiment would have interfered in the evolutionary process of any pre-existing civilization.

Earth called out, her *wam* (the musical "signature" of the soul) permeating every level of consciousness in the Cosmos. Earth's music played undisturbed in the heavens, for no advanced indigenous civilization had ever taken root upon her virgin soil. There was neither the hum nor the static that now resonates out from Gaia. There were only the higher harmonics of her resonant vibratory frequencies and the sure, steady drumming of her heartbeat.

The throat chakra of your solar system, she was identified as the perfect communication center of your quadrant of the material universe by intelligence far beyond your world, those who gazed upon the blue-green planet from a distance and saw that yours was, indeed, a Garden of Eden.

Earth was unexplored territory, a remote planet primed in every possible sense to receive the evolutionary trigger that would catapult her up the spiral. As the Council investigated further, its members observed that, despite its multiform fauna, lush flora, and abundant minerals, the third planet out from Ra's fiery core seemed to be making very little progress towards the development of an intelligent species. For well over a million years, the "ape-man" *Homo erectus* continued to walk the Earth, never seeming to evolve beyond a relatively savage stage of survival existence in the wild.

Earth was deemed the perfect habitat in which to birth the Golden Race.

It was a "match made in the heavens."

Intensive studies were made of the existing environments of Earth—the distinctive plant and animal kingdoms—and detailed investigations were conducted into how bio-diversity resulted as a reflection of various geophysical and climatic variables. It was discerned that such diversity would provide ideal conditions for the seeding of extraterrestrial species, as their original environments could, in many ways, be replicated in the ecosystems of Earth. And, oh, the bountiful waters! No other planet offered such an abundance of the life-bearing element—the essential resource for life throughout the Universe.

The engineers of the Great Experiment knew that if the weakening of the species' genetic pool were to be avoided, a balance of distinctly diverse genetic codes would have to be introduced into the DNA matrix, so that interbreeding would strengthen the race, rather than weaken it, as is so often the case in other worlds and isolated species. Earth offered the ecological diversity and the resources needed to successfully introduce the variant genetic codes and provide for their incubation.

Here lie the true origins of the four master races on Earth ... so very unique in their make-up, while of a common "galactic" nature and intent.

Unexplained in your archeological and missing-link evolutionist theories is the isolated emergence upon your planet of four distinct seed races. These, we can tell you, are archetypes of master races, whose fundamental genetic material formed the primary "substance" of your race, while the vibrational patterns and sequencing of extra-dimensional beings (those of the higher realms) were woven into the intricate light codes of your incredible twelve-stranded DNA.

The genetic material of these four primary races was united in the blueprint of the species of *Homo sapiens*. While combining the DNA of the four races into one matrix, the master geneticists varied the strains so that the predominant genetic material resulting from a given planetary or stellar frequency would be seeded in those specific Gaian climates that most closely resembled the original environment, which they were convinced would best facilitate the successful development of the prototype. This, we reiterate, was intended to strengthen your genetic pool, for the eventual interbreeding of *Homo sapiens* would, in this way, ensure your survival.

Climate, terrain, and the available resources that would best replicate the conditions of the planets of genetic origin were identified. The splicing of the DNA and the blending of genetic material was, in part, determined by the existence of these bio-sympathetic environments, in which the seed of your greatest ancestors would be "planted."

Just as you, in your selected gardening of trees, plant foods, and flowering flora, take great care to consider the perfect light, soil, and moisture to best facilitate the plant's strong and rapid growth in its new world, so did the master geneticists involved in the seeding go to great lengths in selecting the host environments of Earth.

This is an extremely simplistic explanation of how modern

man developed upon your planet, not only as a species entirely diverse from the animals and the "ape-men," but as one of distinct racial characteristics. But it may help you to imagine how such distinctly different races emerged at different points of the globe, far beyond a time when your written record attempted to account for the incredible diversity of your species. It may help you understand why the Darwinian model fails so desperately to adequately describe the true origins of human evolution, one that will never discover the "missing link"...just as it will never recognize the first *Homo sapiens* as the perfected crystals of distant worlds and dimensions.

Formulating the master genetic coding was a collective effort of those donor races, and light beings from many realms participated in the process. The Family of Light infused the brilliance into the matrix, while the master geneticists grounded you with genetic material of the indigenous earth beings *(Homo erectus),* galvanizing the experiment with love and the intention that the Highest Purpose be served.

The selected primary races were considered prototypical of the elements of Earth, and they held resonance with four primary colors: black, red, white, and yellow. From these, new colors would be blended and, subsequently, new racial characteristics would emerge. This was the original design for your physical, emotional, and mental make-up.

It was the color board of the artist.

There exists a planet at a distant point in your galaxy known as Engan, whose gravitational fields and atmospheric conditions are, in many ways, similar to those of the expanding desert regions of Earth. A hot, dry planet, its limited watershed and scarce rainfall are valued as the ultimate resources, while abundant gold and precious ore layers are of no significance to the populace. Far older than Gaia, Engan has seen the birth and rebirth of countless civilizations, the last of which began to die out around the time of the Starseed Project, when the receding of the planet's oceans, resulting from the destruction of the atmosphere, caused drought conditions that reached unsustainable proportions. What ensued, naturally, were massive deaths, which reduced the population to near extinction.

Approached by the Elders, the Engena were the first to agree to participate in the Great Experiment, for they knew that, in doing so, their seed would live on, in a Utopia where water abounded. The genetic material of the Engena, beings of superior physical strength, sexuality, and vital life force, was added to the genetic pool, and theirs would be the overriding, dominant genetic material of human DNA.

You know this as the Negroid race; you associate the Engena with the color black.

The Engena-dominant prototype of *Homo sapiens* was deposited in the hotter climates of Earth's diverse ecosystems, those which most closely resembled their arid, hot planet: the primary locations were the continent of Africa and the Pan-Asian Rim, including Australia and island clusters of the region.

The second master race—the Atl—was a highly evolved civilization from the Pleiades star system, a stellar constellation located at the epicenter of your galaxy. You know their descendents as "red-skins." They joined in the seeding of your great planet to bring the gift of unconditional love into the human matrix. Their participation in the Great Experiment ensured that the sacred heart was anchored within you; it established your incredible capacity for compassion for all life and your ability to exchange that energy with all the living beings of creation.

They were seeded in those lands that evolved into the lost continent of Atlantis, there where mighty peaks and mountains define the horizon. Their modern-day descendants still can be found in the snow-covered lands and the high plains of Earth: in the Tibetan Himalayas, the Andes, the Rockies … and they are the Eskimos, Tibetans, Peruvians, the Maya, and the Natives of the Americas.

The third master race, that which you would identify in the Asian populations (the yellow people), finds its roots at a great distance from your solar system, upon a planet well beyond NASA's current awareness and far from their telescopic reach. Remote and isolated, this ancient planet of origin was, in many ways, in a crisis similar to that of your contemporary world.

Conditions of severe overpopulation and the deification of their sophisticated technological resources had brought the civilization to the final apex point, where they were simply self-destructing. As an unconscious unit of living beings, they had so given their power to that technology that they arrived at that evolutionary chasm into which the human race is now slipping—a world of increasingly powerful robotics and declining mind. They had been seeking to integrate with other worlds (to escape themselves, in a sense) when their intergalactic communications networks picked up the call for the Starseed Project.

They were masters of logic-based communication and technology, true left-brain archetypes. They were seeded in the geographical areas where Earth provided hothouse environments that maintain relatively constant humidity and high temperatures, for that is the ecosystem that best replicates the geophysical elements of their home planet.

The Arien—those you identify as the white race peopling your world—find root in the Orion Constellation. A technologically advanced civilization, they had conquered the obstacles of intergalactic travel and had journeyed far, always reaching further, seeking to understand the vastness of all existence. They were determined explorers, those whose fiery nature drove them always to new shores—curious visionaries of worlds that they had yet to know... and conquer.

They brought into your make-up an overriding will and the desire to excel and dominate as a species. They are the part of you that is forever seeking, that refuses limitation and that thrives upon challenge.

Their planet, fifth out from its central star, was relatively cold, and its sun was colder than yours, so theirs was, in a strictly physical sense, the most delicate genetic material being introduced into the matrix. Their skin was absolutely white, devoid of pigment, and they required almost total shielding from Ra's intense radiation.

The Arien-dominant prototype *Homo sapiens* required the coldest, darkest environments your planet could offer, for else they would never have survived the initial phase of their seeding. They were bred in the temperate lands between the poles of the planet, where oblique rays best replicated those of their own sun and where their extreme geographic isolation would provide the challenges that they needed to survive.

This was the master equation—the four primary elements of your galactic make-up. The Engena (earth), masters of the physical realm, gave you your strength and physical endurance, your procreative force, your survival instinct. The Atl (water) enhanced your ability to love and feel kinship with the living beings around you. The Asians (air) provided your enormous ability to reason and communicate their superior intellect, and Arien consciousness (fire) brought to the seeding the overriding will and the drive to achieve and rise above adversity.

The fifth element, the planetary soul connection, was found in the DNA of *Homo erectus,* Earth's foremost primate. This provided the primordial form and structure of *Homo sapiens,* while grounding you forever to the soul essence of Gaia.

Be wary of applying your current prejudices to these prototypes. **None is superior to the other,** for you are, in almost every way, one and the same. Within each and every one of you lies the genetic material of all four extraterrestrial races—in subtly differing measure. Within you all, as well, is wired the DNA of Light Ones from higher dimensions and that of the indigenous creatures who walked on two feet from the hour of the early dawn, well before *Homo sapiens* was born to Planet Earth.

Viewing this from a Sirian perspective of cosmometric proportion, you recognize that the master geneticists involved in your seeding took great care to honor the sacred directions. The four primary directions *(east, west, north, south)* are represented in the four master races; the *above* in the light codes of the higher realms and the *below* in the slowly evolving ape-man—rooting you to Planet Earth. These elements of cosmic design were carefully united, birthing the seventh direction, the *within* of your being—seat of your soul.

We have touched, only briefly, upon how the four elements of Earth, quintessential aspects of your existence on your planet, are typified in the four root races. These multidimensional constructs must be born in mind as we proceed, for here we are delving into your root consciousness, and you may hear the sound of your ego—that part of you that has been trained and programmed to see the other as different than you—ringing resistant to the reality of your multi-racial, multidimensional, and extraterrestrial make-up.

You are beginning to remember how your race consciousness is rooted in the stars and that your genetic blueprinting includes the DNA of many races. It is a primordial memory, buried deep within your subconscious ... far deeper than your logical minds have been prepared to delve until now.

Such is the reason why most of the human race continues to bear judgment against those who are of another "color." Trapped in the extreme polarity of Earth's fields, most of your race still see the difference rather than the similarity—the mutual development and gifts made manifest through peaceful co-existence and interbreeding. Indeed, you must bear in mind that, were it not for that genetic diversity, the human race simply would not have survived, just as whole populations of flora and fauna have reached extinction in other genetically isolated planetary environments.

The lesson of your racial interdependence should be taught in your schools and spoken in the public arenas, there where the seeds of racial tension are germinated and all too often grow into conflict and rage amongst your youth. The irony of your race-resistance is that your apparent differences are actually your strengths, just as they are your sameness. Your racial diversity is as **necessary** to your survival as the air you breathe and the water you drink. The genetic material introduced into your design was chosen to combine the strengths of some of the most advanced civilizations of the Universe into your make-up, while assuring the very survival of your species.

Risking redundancy, we restate one simple fact. Those of you who still harbor feelings of racial superiority over others should remember that without the darker, lighter, or different one, you most likely would never have made it into the twenty-first century on Planet Earth.

By understanding your true roots—your oneness—you will rediscover the absolute beauty of the other, and you will learn to love that one as part of you.

Then you will recognize the expanding heart of humanity.

Then you will understand the meaning and the value of One.

3

Raping the Nest

While the Light Forces of the Council carefully nested *Homo sapiens* in the warmth of Gaia's nourishing fields, polar forces moved into Earth's orbit to "rob the cradle" of your incubation on what they believed to be their ground ... and theirs alone.

We must go back in history and attempt to describe, briefly, the celestial events that were sculpting the forms of earth reality at the time of the birthing of your race.

As we have previously explained in the Atlantis material, the eccentric planet, Nebiru, careened into your solar system over 450,000 years ago, upon its expulsion from Sirius B—the ascending Solar Deity of our triunal stellar system.* Celestial mechanics created a dynamic whereby Nebiru would continue to reenter the body of your system at approximately 3,600-year intervals and then journey back to the outer fields of Sirius, from whence it would then be bounced back again ... in an endless circuit between the two star systems.

The Annunaki (rulers of Nebiru) first came into contact with Earth at that time, and like so many others who have discovered new worlds, they celebrated a new land—one they believed would lead to their salvation. This you must understand about

---

* See *Atlantis Rising: The Struggle of Darkness and Light.*

the Annunaki and their later intervention in the Starseed Project: they, residents of a planet lost (in a sense) in space, saw Earth, a biologically inviting environment, as an eventual solution to their inevitable extinction.

Their "Manifest Destiny" approach to Earth conquest was no different than your Secret Government's current plans to invade other realms in space, for your modern rulers (descendants of the Annunaki) are no less arrogant than their great ancestors in their belief that other worlds are there for the taking.

Indeed, it is history in the "remaking."

Like your current explorers' missions in space, the Annunaki's first landing teams were initially interested in mining Earth for its wealth of energy-producing minerals and ores—resources that would be essential to their survival out in the dark space between Sirius and Ra. Only later, when they realized that their home planet, Nebiru, was doomed to extinction, did they develop a plan to evacuate their leaders and the family elite and slowly rebuild their civilization upon Gaian soil.

This has been recounted in greater detail in the second book of the Trilogy, *Atlantis Rising*. There we have described the celestial events that first drew Nebiru into your solar system. Let us reproduce this information here for you, so that you may have a clearer understanding of how they have moved into your reality and become entwined in human evolution:

> *Once Nebiru moved close enough into range that they could effect a full-scale probe of the planet, the Annunaki boarded their "great sailing ships" and moved in for a closer look, surprised to find a remote, undevel-*

oped planet—bursting with unlimited plant and animal species—with no visible signs of an intelligent civilization.

This, to beings of the much older star system of Sirius, was a revolutionary discovery. It was foreign to their perception of a Universe known to be teeming with intelligent life that a host planet of such rich resources had not yet been cultivated by a sentient species—one at least superior to the animals they encountered during their first landing missions.

They left Planet Earth to its natural evolutionary process, hoping to see great leaps in your progress with each return into your solar system, for they knew that one day they would need intelligent life forms to produce energy for them. Nonetheless, to the Annunaki, Earth was now their private real estate, and they set their intention to develop the property, checking in on its progress from time to time, as was facilitated by their new course through the 3D universe.

With each cyclical reentry into the body of Ra, the Nebiruans discovered more about the planets that joined Earth in their orbit around your Sun. As with Mars, they did investigate and colonize other celestial bodies in the solar system, but you were always the target and focus of their interest, for Earth was the most appetizing. They observed the changing face of Gaia, studying the flora and fauna of her vast virgin lands. Like curious scientists, they occasionally intervened in Earth's process with technologies that belonged to your future, mutating the natural

*progression of the life forms that abounded at that stage
to fit their future needs of the planet.*

*At a much later point in their many returns to the far
reaches of our stellar body, they got wind of the Great
Experiment being planned for Gaia and became outraged.
They believed that we were interfering in their territorial
domain, for they had watched and waited for Earth to
reach the point where they could harvest her resources, and
they had their own ideas for genetic intervention on Earth.
These involved potentially mixing their own seed with that
of the primate,* Homo erectus, *to create an intelligent brute
force to mine and work the Earth for them.*

*Indeed, their first experiments had been promising.
When news of the successful seeding of* Homo sapiens,
*the super race of light beings, reached their sentinels, it
was decided that the only way they would retain control
over their new domain was by sabotaging the new human
race, so that they might drive our attention away from
Planet Earth forever.*

*It may shock you to hear that the first extraterrestrial
abductions occurred one hundred thousand years ago,
when the Annunaki teams descended upon the Earth and
rewired your DNA, disabling ten of the twelve strands
that were part of your original make-up: your light coding. You were raped of your immense potential, stripped to
the bare bones required for your survival as a race and as
future subjects of Annunaki rule. Their intentions for your
planet simply did not allow for a sudden, super race of
multidimensional beings upsetting their plans of an eventual takeover of the planet.*

Obviously, they knew that those who had birthed you were, in a sense, attending to your incubation in the warm nest of Gaia's light. In those halcyon days of your emergence, Homo sapiens, *the Light Ones of the Universe were focused upon you, celebrating your future as the new curators of the solar system in which you reside, for it was your destiny to reach greatness within and beyond the limits of your realm.*

They, the Annunaki, knew we would respond to their invasive act—the sabotaging of the Great Experiment—but they were in a position to act quickly. Once the biogeneticists had completed their mission, their engineers threw the grid around the planet, an immense force field that created such dissonant waves that, in fact, we found we were unable to reach resonance with you. Although, with time, we have been able to adjust our frequency to penetrate the weakening field and get through to growing numbers of you, the grid still surrounds your world, and it continues to plague you. It has caused great disruption of the Earth, while disturbing you on many levels . . . particularly there, where it interacts with Gaia's own electromagnetic vortex point.

Can you truly conceive of it: a multidimensional Universe of dark and light forces, in which galactic beings of every shape and vibration have actually set the course of human destiny?

We are telling you that the story of your very birth is, in significant ways, a reflection of numerous "alien" civilizations. Of these, there are so many shades of reality and so many shades of being. Everywhere there are polar opposites (diminishing as one climbs the spiral of return to the Godhead), souls in transition, souls in transformation, the birth of alien nations, the death of others.

You have reached the point where you are becoming consciously aware of where you come from, and that, Dear Ones, is a most significant key to understanding where you are headed, for the journey is not one of directions, nor does it reflect your understanding of that ubiquitous and pervading aspect of your limitation in 3D: time. It is one of progression: from darkness to light, from matter to light, from crystal to light...lighter still—to the ecstatic return, when all consciousness eventually merges back to Source.

This is the absolute truth of Creation, of all existence and of the very nature of life in every form, at every juncture of the Universe: the All That Is, That Ever Was, and That Always Will Be.

4

The Roots of Racism

Here you are, *Homo sapiens,* one hundred thousand years old by that earthly clock with which you measure the passage of time. The primary colors of your starseeded ancestry have blended into new hues and tonalities, as even the most remote pockets of indigenous earth peoples have been sucked into the mainstream, and the spiral of human evolution swirls into a homogenous commonality.

The borders of your geographic isolation have all but fallen away. Mass migration and interbreeding of incredible numbers of people from the far corners of your world have drawn you together, as was foreseen by our Elders and the master geneticists who contributed their genius to the Starseed Project.

Yet, consciousness of racial diversity permeates almost every layer of your civilization, its roots far more deeply ingrained within you than you can consciously imagine or understand— based upon the misinformation and lies that have been embedded in the fabric of human history and the discordant frequencies that have, for so long, been resounding through the Earth realm.

Deep, deep within you lies the memory of your starseed, for all the cells of your being resonate to the wam vibrations of your stellar homes, just as they connect you to Earth. That primordial memory is laced throughout the crystallized fiber of your complex double-helix DNA material, just as it is keyed into the ten additional etheric filaments that have lain dormant within the human genetic codex **until now.**

Many of you are beginning to reactivate and rebundle these mutating DNA codes, aided by cosmic energies filtering into Earth's fields and the immensely amplified radiation of your Solar Deity, which the propaganda has you fearing ... while you cover yourselves in harmful (and enormously profitable) chemical shields of the "sun tanning" variety.

More of you are now intent upon accelerating the process of your DNA mutation, which is why we are dedicated to assisting you through the work of our instrument and others like her, who are serving as the voice of extradimensional influences dedicated to serving humankind.

Here you must be discerning, for there is much misinformation circulating regarding the process—from the method to the ramifications—and you will need to bring forward that inner sense of what is right for you. You will need to examine ego levels (both your own and those of the guides who propose to work with you), expectations, and promises.

You will need to be grounded in truth and integrity.

The activation of a third strand of DNA is of paramount significance to your ascension process, since its reassembly creates triangulation within the DNA—the resolution of duality and your leap of consciousness from a three-dimensional orientation into far more complex cosmometric proportions. These will bring you into resonance with significant other alternate realities, dimensions, and universes. Indeed, the heightened cellular consciousness that evolves from the activation of the etheric third strand is either beginning now or will eventually take form in the sea of your body matter. It will manifest in exquisite crystalline formations that represent, both in their physical and etheric frequencies, the complex star tetrahedron, microcosm of the merkaba energy fields which define the "I am" awareness of every element of your being and your interconnectedness to the celestial deities, the Earth Mother, and all that lies beyond your immediate fields of awareness.

These perfect formations, the templates around which the remaining strands of DNA will eventually crystallize, are the manifestation of your expanding awareness. As your free scientists bring forward the evidence, you will realize with what splendor and intricate cosmometry higher consciousness crystallizes within every cell, facilitating your rapid transmutation. It is our intention to elaborate these patterns of your evolving cellular consciousness—the blueprint of all Creation—in depth as we progress through these transmissions.

Others, whose spiritual progression is far more advanced in this phase of their soul journey, are experiencing the reassembly of the secondary triangulation: the fourth, fifth, and sixth strands. This genetic "rewiring" is plugging them back in to their galactic circuitry—reconnecting them to their respective star systems and flooding their bodies and all that surrounds them with light.

As you can well imagine, this has everything to do with why so many are now attuning to the frequencies that enable them to bring through extraterrestrial and extradimensional communications from the Family of Light.

Another aspect of mutating human DNA is manifest in the birth of growing numbers of exceptional children, who have been incarnating in these most recent years of your transformation. A new soul collective, entering with the Supraluminescence of nine fully interactive strands, is bringing in an extraordinary new awareness to help the dormant emerge from the chrysalis and take flight. These are the Children of the Violet Oversoul, Light Ones who have committed to entering the earth arena long enough to help your race transmute form and transcend the limitations of your vibrational entrainment for once and forever.

Know that these are "first time" visitors to the Earth realm, and they carry no karmic baggage, for they are evolved souls who have volunteered to assist in your ascension process by retrograding back into the third dimension to perform a quite specific mission for Gaia and for the living of your world. Light-bodied beings who had long ago completed the cyclical process of incarnation in the physical realm, they agreed to reenter with the third triangulation of DNA (the Trinity exalted) to serve as ascension models and to remind you of your potential, once the controls over Planet Earth have been released and you are, once again, receptive and fully awake.

Most have surmounted the difficulties of holding the original DNA "wiring" by selecting birth locations corresponding to the weakest points of the electromagnetic grid surrounding your planet—where not even the most sophisticated Annunaki technology is strong enough to disrupt the cosmic river of higher consciousness flowing into your space. It is in these locations, understandably, that the cosmic waves traversing your solar system are most powerful and where acceleration is being experienced by greater numbers of you.

Their appearance at these key locations is amplifying the light of awakening earth awareness, while serving to neutralize and disband the electromagnetic grid, which, for so long, has plagued you. We will be telling you more about these highly psychic, cosmically attuned children—the Violet Oversoul—and their imminent move into leadership roles in the heat of the Desert Days. We will explain to you just how they will be guiding humankind through the valley of fear and onto higher ground.

It is important to remember that the dark forces—those that hover in the ethers and those that walk the ground of Gaia—are masters of frequency and they have broadband communication with earth beings. Their essence permeates the lower astral, just as it is aired across the wires and transmitters of your global communications networks.

A number of declared channelers amongst you have, often unwittingly, attuned to these lower energies, and their message is not of the highest intention. Therefore, be discerning, for not all who purport to bring through otherworldly communications are necessarily working with light beings.

We see that many of you are dangerously susceptible, for you so long to reconnect with the Family, and that hope—that innate human curiosity—opens you to any number of entities who would feed upon your energies and find expression through your voice. There are astral entities hovering in the ethers, just as there are human beings who have chosen to linger in the shadows, and **you will be tested.**

They would love to hook into you, above all, to drink of the boundless energy that flows from the fountains of your souls.

Your ego centers are the access points through which these lower energies are able to reach and attach to you, so should you feel yourselves swelling with a sense of self-importance—a glorification of your talents and gifts—you may need to pay particularly close attention to the source of your "enlightenment."

You must be wary—so terribly wary—of the ego-self.

Use your discerning intellect to question the intention of all that enters your field of consciousness, and your intuition will provide the answers. Learn to filter all information by calling upon your guides to encircle you in the white light, and then, in the full brilliance of Spirit, you can be free to bring it in, embracing what you know in your hearts to be truth and willing that the rest be bounced back to its source. This form of spiritual clearing is essential to your personal experience.

Above all, be honest with yourselves, immaculate in your intent, for it is of the utmost importance that you be grounded in truth if you are to declare yourselves messengers and warriors of the light.

Remember, too, that what is true for you may not be for another, and that also is a matter of free will, which must always be honored and respected at every level.

⁘⁘⁙⁘⁘

The Power ruling Earth, hybrid descendants of select Annunaki/ Atlantean interbreeding, want to deny you all access to the story of your true origins, for they know that such empowering realizations will shake you from their clutches. They want to prevent the acceleration of your transmutation into light body, whereby you reassemble your original genetic "wiring," for they are fully aware that you are soon to release from limitation and soar beyond your confinement.

They know it … and yet they are determined that, by increasing the pressure of their control mechanisms, they will be able to hold the human race in submission, so that they may continue (for the time they have left) to use you as their servants and slaves—their most valuable resource.

Why? The answer should be obvious. It is because you produce incredible wealth for them; you serve as their brute force; you destroy, kill, and die for them; you feed their ego centers; you give them great power over you, stimulating their killer instincts. Moreover, you provide them with possibilities for their own survival that, without you, would never exist. That process is described in great detail in *Atlantis Rising,* and it is important that you access that information. It will help you understand the motivation that drives the Power, and it may stir within you feelings of compassion and forgiveness—expressions of your expanding humanity.

This is how you arise from the darkness and release yourselves from the clutches of those who would impede your passage.

By holding humankind in absolute survival mode, they are assured that you function in full capacity as their technicians, warriors and slaves. By stimulating your sexual libido and physical desire, they can entrap you in predictable behavior modes and steer you into the darker corners of human emotion.

We are pleased to see how many of you are immune to such manipulations, for you are centered in the heart, from where unconditional love passes between you and into Gaia. You are empowered with the perennial light of love and the knowing that you are sovereign beings—souls upon the pathway.

From the absolute center of your being, you see light in the other—your own reflection—and by the nature of that expression you understand the connection. You walk in the light of your higher selves. You become **invincible.**

The mass population, however, is deliberately stimulated to see the difference of the other—and to fear or hate those differences. This alienation is most overtly experienced as race distinction, although the lines of separation that have been drawn between you are, clearly, not of a racial nature alone. Still, the greater body of earth beings, unaware of the power structures that have been put into place to control the human race, is still being manipulated into feelings of racial paranoia. It is this root prejudice that holds the majority in separation and alienation.

As the awakening of Earth join hands to raise the vibration, you are finding that, despite the intentions of the covert forces, the destructive patterns of racial discrimination are, in fact, disappearing in your personal lives and communal consciousness. It is nonsense; it is darkness manifest. Your release from the constraints of the time enigma and the illusions of the material realm—your emergence—are inconsonant with such negative and wasteful energies.

Your ability to discern the mechanisms of race consciousness is essential to your unification, and it is time that you pay great attention to how it is stimulated within you, so that the process of racial segregation that still haunts humankind can no longer operate at subliminal levels and more of you can interact in the light of mutual acceptance and unconditional love.

As you feel expansion of the heart center, swelling with the light of so many kindred souls, you embrace the true meaning of your existence and achieve a universal connection to all life—multi-dimensional consciousness. You celebrate your diversity and uniqueness, knowing that all have contributed to the whole—the enrichment of the human race and the strengthening of the genetic pool. You experience the One Heart, as it beats the rhythm of the heavens, warmed in the knowing that no matter how vast your differences, you are all children of the stars.

All are starseed.

Race consciousness and discrimination on your planet have always been orchestrated by the Secret Government, which wants to distract you with discordant human emotions to render you more manageable as a mass, holding you focused on the ridiculous so that your desire to question the far more serious issues facing your race will wane.

Consider that they are a mere two thousand individuals, and you are six billion. What would happen if the entire human population were to rise up against them? You can be certain that those who form the "think tank" organizations, whose role it is to manage Earth and the global population, spend much of their time deliberating on how delicately they hold power over you and how easily that ratio could backlash against them—rendering their insidious designs useless as the storm of human consciousness took back what has been taken away.

There are numerous methods used to hold you in obedience, applied since the earliest days of your birth as earth beings. There is an order to the process of possessing the human race, a most simplistic pattern, which is known in the inner circles of the Secret Government as "The Recipe." This is comprised of seven essential "ingredients" for stirring human emotion into desired behavioral blends of obedience, resignation, and submission. They are:

- "Disconnecting" ten of the twelve light-coded filaments of human DNA, achieved through the activation of the electromagnetic grid placed around Planet Earth. (These dissonant frequencies scattered cosmic light waves and disrupted the Gossamer Web, so that the Family of Light could no longer reach you.)
- Manipulating earth frequencies to hold the planet in imbalance, accentuating three-dimensional polarity.
- Holding the races in isolation from all extra-planetary intelligence, while separating them from **each other.**
- Encouraging their division by race, sex, religion, and community; stimulating hate, fear, prejudice, and resentment in the base human emotional frequencies.
- Feeding their animal selves through the survival and sexuality centers—through entrainment, subliminal manipulation, and mind control.

- Creating false leaders—icons in whom the masses will place their trust when things are proceeding well and blame when they are not.
- Rewarding the obedient, punishing the rebellious.

As elementary as it seems (for surely we cannot claim to explain away the woes of the human race in "seven easy steps"), these remain the general parameters of control that are still being used against you—as they have been throughout human history. It is our intention, in these transmissions, to elucidate these aspects in greater detail, for they are the foundation of the secrets and lies that must now be burned in effigy—their ashes scattered and healed in the cosmic sea of All That Is.

Consider what we have told you about the four master races and how the magnificent union of those genetic elements within you forms the essence of human nature. You have physical might (the survival instinct), a great capacity for love and intense emotion, an exquisite intellect, and the drive to achieve greatness... to master the Universe. You have the fifth element, the grounding seed: your Gaian chord. You have the sixth—the higher consciousness of the Family of Light—dormant within you, awaiting the awakening of what has always been yours.

Think about how these aspects of your entirety form the greater whole of humanity and how all contribute to the magnificence of *Homo sapiens*.

Bear in mind that alienating you from each other (and from the Galactic Community) is essential to the stimulation of your ego-consciousness, where you perform their deeds for the gratification of the self . . . for the "rewards." Know that perpetuation of race distinction is deliberate and that the pockets of extremists that plague your societies (the so-called "skinheads," separatists, and segregationists) are covertly financed and instigated as part of a highly organized central scheme. They, the visible disrupters, are key elements in the design of human isolation—warriors for the Power.

Of these, some are well aware that the architecture of racial hatred is simple management strategy, while others have been programmed to truly believe in the superiority of races and religions—nurturing their blind visions as "insights."

Consider the arrival of the one believed by many to be "Satan" incarnate: Adolf Hitler. Indeed, he has been crystallized in your group consciousness as the Antichrist—archetype of all that which is evil in your world.

This was an individual who brought into the incarnation baggage of the darkest substance—karma accumulated in a most painfully repetitive return to form, for this soul chose to cling to the shadows and to reap the material rewards of such choices—if "rewards" they can be called. We suggest that he was a perfect candidate for induction into the Secret Government's army—warriors against peace and freedom for the beings of Planet Earth.

The Hitler construct of hate and racial supremacy has been and is still being stimulated within you deliberately, kept alive just as much by those who have suffered at his hand as by the "neo-Nazis" who have been programmed to rekindle worship of those dark icons. Your contemporary historical record, the tales of World War II, are impregnated with the stench of the death of the innocent, victims of the cruelest intention and human indecency.

The Jewish population has collectively committed to bringing the story forward, from generation to generation, for eternity. We understand their indignation and contempt, for it was they, more than any other ethnic minority, who bore the violence of his rage. However, we wish to suggest that your modern civilization's determination never to let go of the memory (whether born from the hate of the executioner or of a renewed worship of the dark hero) only tethers you to the violent intention, accentuating the Hitler vibration and fortifying its etheric imprint.

It is a cord that is better broken.

All war is cruel and indecent and, without wishing in any way to minimize the injustice perpetrated upon the victims of Hitler, we ask you to remember that war, the violent exchange between semiconscious beings, is at the same time an act of collective unconscious. To rouse you to kill the other, the Power stimulates within you distinctions of race, religion, and behaviors of separation; this is achieved by activating the "animal" within you—often through the use of subliminal technology.

You are programmed to believe that your survival, your root belief structures, your emotional gratification, and your (sense of) power are threatened by those who are "different" from you. You are corralled into nations, religions, racial segments—even neighborhoods—and made to believe in the illusion that this is union, the organization of like-beings, in which you find identity and strength.

What you may not want to believe is that the Hitlers of the

world only arrive at such power because the Authority recognizes their charismatic capacities, for they serve to stimulate mass consciousness into fear and powerlessness. That is how the Power manages to keep billions of beings under the control of but a few thousand. Like the corrupt politicians of your contemporary governments, Adolf Hitler was financed by the Secret Government to do its dirty work, while performing a sort of test run of the One World Government, which (as you know) is taking form now... in the dress rehearsal of *The Greatest Show on Earth,* now "showing" in the global theater.

There is much more to the Hitler conspiracy than you realize—much more than you have been led to believe about the cause and effect of his brutal offensive. The official story is untrue: Hitler was not a raving madman, as he is almost always portrayed. Nor was he the lone architect of the reign of terror that defines the epoch of his walking upon the Earth. Rather, he was a skilled manipulator and an important tool of the Power—as were his allies in the lands of Nippon and fascist Italy. He was a knight of the Secret Government, a player on the global power board.

Hitler came up from the ranks of secret societies that provided him awesome financial backing—the kind that transcends your national borders. We are telling you that he had funding that extended well beyond the vaults of the Dark Alliance. Do not believe the "good guys" propaganda that has been fed to you to justify your part in that war, and the deaths of so many innocent husbands, brothers, and sons. Adolf Hitler was free to reach into the Secret Government's endless pot of gold, for he was commissioned to play the part of the Satan, as are your contemporary supervillains—for these are continually being created to convince you of your vulnerability.

A worshipper of dark forces, Hitler attuned to the darkest aspects of occult magic, developing his abilities to manifest those energies in the material—a true black magician. He was well-trained by the power elite in the use of mind-control technologies, and you have yet to fully understand how the application of subliminal frequencies and images were used to mesmerize and manipulate his armies and the citizenry—inciting their nationalistic fervor and obedience. These were used, as well, to create the narcotic of resignation that rendered his enemies passive enough to be taken and the people drugged enough to allow it.

This aspect of subconscious submission has never been duly elaborated in the history books, for the techniques that achieved these responses are still a very active part of the manipulations that are being conducted upon the global society. They are still **secret.** The writers of the books—the chroniclers of the Secret Government—are not commissioned to bring you truth. They are perpetrators of the lies that are used, throughout history, to sway the masses and to cement false images in the collective unconscious.

Hitler had access to the emerging technologies that are now sweeping your world, but fortunately they were still in the birthing (or rebirthing) stage. These involved genetic manipulation, Tesla warfare, biological, chemical, and atomic weaponry, and his dream: the cloning of the Aryan prototype to establish white supremacy on Planet Earth. He was commissioned, in a sense, to serve as a sort of test pilot of the New World Order that was being prepared for this stage of your civilization, when (it was foreseen) the human population was expected to explode into five billion.

You have exceeded those calculations by more than one billion beings; this the Government realized years before it created the AIDS virus.

Whereas Hitler's assignment was the extermination of the Jewish population, the current massacre of life on your planet—a massive covert viral and bacterial war—has a far greater scope. This population-reduction program first targeted homosexuals, drug users, and black populations of Africa. Today, as they intended, AIDS has taken such hold in the global arena that we observe one out of seven individuals is already infected—and those odds are soon to be even more dramatically stacked against you.

If you have difficulty accepting the idea that a lethal virus has been deliberately introduced into society to reduce your numbers, then you are going to have a hard time comprehending just what is in store for you now that a One World Order has passed the testing phase and is now being openly imposed upon the global society.

As for the evil villain, Hitler, let us set the record straight as to his "tragic end." He did not die trapped in his lair by the declared heroes, nor did he suicide with his Aryan lover—that story is sheer fabrication. Would a man so obsessed with totalitarian power have left his own survival to chance, overlooking a simple escape plan? Moreover, would such a personality—one whose ego demanded absolute supremacy over all others—resort to the cowardly act of suicide?

No, the record is wrong.

Or rather, as some of you are discovering…**it is a lie.**

We remind you that penetration of the subsurface has been under way since as far back as Atlantis, where elaborate energy stations were part of an extensive underground network. These plans are still in the hands of the Secret Government.

Military bases, laboratories, and underground communities literally line your planet and are, today, headquarters for untold covert scientific and military operations. Nuclear launch stations, on twenty-four hour emergency status, openly operate below Cheyenne Mountain in the region known as Colorado: authorized media have even been allowed to enter and conduct interviews there—just to let you know how the cards are stacked against you. Similar bases dot the entire globe.

Other installations of the underground, such as the controversial site referred to as "Area 51," are to remain relatively secret, for the nature of their investigations into extraterrestrial craft and anti-gravity propulsion is still being denied you.

Hitler's Nazi headquarters and its access to secret tunnels have been touched upon in the documenting of World War II, but little has been made known as to just where those secret passageways led. Some suggest that these were used as "escape routes," and that is partially correct. We reiterate that it was not the dead bodies of Adolf and his "Eve" that were found at the "suicide scene." The construction of the death scene was carefully designed; their devoted "doubles" were murdered to provide the corpses—to convince the world that the evil sorcerer and his witch were dead at last and that "good" had triumphed over evil.

Before the seizure of Hitler's private bunker, there had been frequent passages through the secret corridors of the underground, for they led to key subsurface military installations of Secret Government operatives. There, in the shadowy world of the subsurface, there are no nations ... there are no borders. We ask you to consider that when you think about enemies and heroes, about the "good" and "bad" world leaders.

Hitler lived another twenty years in the underground, serving the Power by contributing his strategic genius to the plans for the New World Order, and he added considerably to your current global dilemma—while assuring that his memory (and vibration) live on.

Let us suggest that the collective consciousness that has made of Hitler an archetypal supervillain has also created the new Nazis. They are fueled by the hatred and loathing of his mid-century victims, and we wonder when you, a conscious society, are you going to let go of him. With what we have told you of resonance, you should understand how the dark energies and lower emotions linked to the memory actually connect you to him—fortifying that dark vibration on every level.* Remember that like energies attract, and that your hatred of the tyrant resonates with his darkest thoughts ... which, we remind you, still hang in the ethers.

Only when you can forgive the models of darkness can you move onto higher ground. Only then will the grotesque shadow pale and eventually fade away.

Perhaps it will give you pause for consideration that the Power

---

* See *Atlantis Rising,* chapter seven.

perpetuates the Hitler story so that you will augment that dark vibration with your resentment, your sense of victimization and loathing.

Ethnic cleansing is a most incomprehensible evil, and to forgive the despots of death is no easy task. Lest you forget, however, the heroic side of that war bears a tarnished star for, despite the media's avoidance of the nuclear question, you must remember that the Western Alliance did elect the "final" option for the helpless populations of Hiroshima and Nagasaki.

They did annihilate and kill the innocent there.

Your parents believed the "no other choice" excuse for that omnipotent act, as if the constructed enemy attack upon the hallowed grounds of American soil—the Pearl Harbor incident—could in any way justify the final response: the detonation of such a force upon all the living things of that world. Never forget that your leaders had to rouse the population to such a point that they could justify their entering the war and the eventual detonation of their new, "secret" nuclear weapon upon an entire population—the once great enemy nation known to you as "Japan."

We find your conscious sidestepping of that significant occurrence a most extraordinary example of how you are managed by the Power. While the Hitler story resounds endlessly across the waves of human conscious, almost nowhere does one find reference to the atomic devastation unleashed by the "good guys" of that war. Do you understand how your perception of the unfolding events of your world are molded of fabrication and the distortion of truth?

You—lightworkers of Gaia—have come to help penetrate

the smokescreens and clear the way for your passage from the Desert Days into the no-time. This is a process of operating in correct mind and action. It is about getting at the secret story and extracting it from the blanket of lies that has been wrapped around your world.

It is about living in truth.

It begins with forgiveness and travels on the waves of unconditional love.

5

Who Really Rules the Earth?

It does not take an expert in mathematical logistics to recognize that the ratio between two thousand top Secret Government overlords and six billion human beings overwhelmingly favors **you** as the true rulers of Earth—by your sheer numbers, if not your collective mind power. There are three million of you to every one member of the power elite **(3,000,000: 1),** and yet they, an absolute minority, still manage to secretly rule over the entire planet. Their imposed supremacy over you is, by any reasonable standard, a mathematical improbability—a totally unnatural occurrence in the biological sequencing of all life on your planet. And yet, they have managed ... throughout history ... to do it.

Just who these individuals are, truthfully, is irrelevant. Some are totally sheathed in the dark sepulchers of total anonymity— vampires sucking the blood of humanity; others are only semi-veiled in the protective mantle of extraordinary wealth and power. We suggest that you focus more upon how they operate—how they manipulate human behavior—and less upon pointing fingers and naming names, which serves nothing more than to increase your paranoia and distract you from the far greater concerns posed by their lordship over the human race.

It is dangerous to be setting out on a "witch-hunt" where cauldrons are a-brew, so be prudent and, above all, Dear Ones . . . **stay focused.**

Much more important is that you understand the mechanisms of abusive power, for you can transform them when you heighten your awareness and consciously reclaim your right to sovereignty as individuals and, moreover, as a people. You are brilliant when you exercise your free will to think and act of your own volition, declaring in every moment of your lives that you intend that the higher purpose be served on every level . . . and that the good of the All be integrated into every thought and action.

We offer you this protective shield, a mantra that resounds throughout the free-will zones of the Universe. Let it become part of your daily regime and mental hygiene:

> *"I am a sovereign being*
> *exercising free will as I ascend the spiral of Spirit;*
> *I intend that the Higher Purpose be served and*
> *that the light Prevail . . ."*

We are telling you that nothing can overpower you if you stand tall in your clarity and purpose. You can deflect negativity, shining bright the light of your evolving spirit, or you can resonate to it through disempowering thoughts and emotions.

Do you see the potential that is held in the hands of the manipulators? How you, as individuals, perceive the dynamics of imposed power and the human response is fundamental to the cause and effect of those dynamics upon the greater whole. Remember . . . each of you bears responsibility for the entirety, for, as units of the global population, you radiate out enormous emotional fields, just as you reflect those of "the other" all around your world, and just as those pass into and through you.

What the Secret Government has over you—more than its impressive technology, secret knowledge, and unfathomable wealth—is its indivisibility, for it operates as an impenetrable unit, while most human beings are focused on their most immediate personal agendas. You have been trained and programmed to think in individualistic terms, for the Power knows that such is the nexus of rule. They know that as long as they can hold the human race in ego-centered consciousness, they can be assured their long-standing reign over you.

There lie the sum and substance of your power struggle.

They can stimulate your alienation one from the other and from the Earth with utterly insignificant classifications, polarizing you into separate religions, nations, races, and an endless array of opposing belief structures. They know how to activate the animal, to drug and addict you, dividing and isolating you from each other and desensitizing your community awareness—as it suits their purposes. They are just as clever at driving you to nationalistic frenzy, creating false loyalties to the superheroes, when those illusions are required.

While many of you still experience yourselves in limiting ideologies and emotions that strictly regard your own lives and those of your immediate families, they view you as the "masses," dissecting you into nations and opposition camps of various credos and cultures. They cultivate your sense of alienation from government, from your societies, and from each other, feeding you doomsday material and scenes of the lowest forms of human behavior through their media—the global "voice."

Anaesthetized, people stare into their television screens, resigned to the desperation of those they see starving and dying in worlds just beyond their comfort zones. Yet, in successive frames, they are stimulated into feelings of envy and unworthiness at not being as fashionably underweight as the "sex object" model in the paid advertisement, one of the many that finances the evening news—where real people are dying of hunger.

We find such paradox quite a statement of the human condition.

Most think in terms of being more "fortunate," "safer," or more "worthy"—such measures only create a sense of separation from the "other."

It is not your destiny, *Homo sapiens,* to devolve into a robotic race of desensitized, insecure TV-entrained creatures, nor are the values portrayed on your screens those you intended to pursue when your souls decided to crystallize, once again, in Earth's fields. This is not a true reflection of human potential!

Observe the children more closely. Few are those who escape the indoctrination of video-stimulated brain patterning, for most of you accept that this is simply the way of the new generation. We assure you that the road to excellence of mind and spirit lies far from the numbing mechanisms that are overtaking your societies, diverting your attention—suppressing the enormous capacities of the intuitive and intellectual minds.

Fortunately, there are many, like you, who are awakening—committed to raising global consciousness. We are pleased to see that you are only marginally affected by the tools of the Power. This diversity demonstrates how the free-will decisions of all individuals determine whether they will drown in the apathy that is being inculcated within the human race or stand their ground against the polar forces of darkness.

We wish to rouse the sleeping from hibernation and help draw them out of the dark caves, where they have been fooled into believing they can weather the winter of social decline. This, as the process of ascension accelerates and the entire human race faces the transmutational fury of Gaian energies, is of great importance to your "future."

Will you join us? Will you, harbingers of the New Light that shines at the Equinox of your rebirthing, help us draw the beast from its lair?

⁂

As for those who comprise the true inner core of the Secret Government, it is untrue that they are warring within their factions. This is deliberate misinformation, designed to mislead those of you who have become more aware of their presence and who are bringing that awareness to the populace. They know that if they can get you thinking of them as individuals, rather than as a consolidated force, you will then apply your own separatist expressions of the human experience to your impressions of them—and that, Dear Ones, will diffuse the power that you derive from your growing awareness of their existence.

We will elaborate the covert technologies at work against human spirit in transmissions that follow. Our concern here is that, as members of the global society, you understand and accept your responsibility for what is unfolding in earth events, for you must never forget that, despite the covert manipulations and subliminal controls of the Secret Government, **you are free-will beings.**

You have only to consider the true leaders of past and contemporary societies, who represent the quintessence of human spirit—those who could not and cannot be bought off with material rewards and animal pleasures and so are silenced and brought to obedience. So illuminating are they that the mere attempt to shadow their light only intensifies it, just as the eclipsed Sun draws all eyes to its searing brilliance. There are brilliant spirit leaders, such as the Bodhisattva Dalai Lama, who are models of compassion and inner clarity. There are others, such as Mahatma Gandhi and Martin Luther King, who have shown you how resounding can be the voice of your unity and peaceful rebellion. Still others have demonstrated how the exquisite human intellect, intensified by enormous social commitment and compassion for the human condition, can break down the walls of your confinement. And there are the lightworkers amongst you, working on so many levels to heal the dark spaces and illuminate the greater society through their work at the individual, communal, and international levels.

Consider the purchasing power of six billion pennies, one distributed to every soul upon your planet. That which, as an entirety, would amount to sixty million dollars (a potentially significant amount—one that could have a significant impact upon some aspect of social or environmental reform) is, at the unitary level, a worthless sum. At the cost of living in most of your "civilized" world, there is almost nothing that can be acquired with one single cent. Not even there, in the poorest of nations, would one penny yield any significant reward.

You see that six billion pennies, distributed one to every single individual of your earth, would barely suffice, say, to sweeten the life of even one child for more than a minute's pleasure at the candy shop. Therefore, you must recognize how the power of a potentially significant "sum of its parts" can be reduced to nothing by means of its division—in a sense, a change in its form. You, the human race, are like those six billion pennies when you operate as separate, ego-centered individuals ... but the potential of your unification—the strength of six billion people—is awe-inspiring.

How possibly could you be dominated if you were united in your intention, always focused upon the ideal that the Highest Purpose being served? The chorus of your one voice would drown out all discord, and the electromagnetic frequencies currently holding reign over you would be disbanded. The Music of the Spheres, your orchestra, would be heard by all.

The force of two thousand would dissipate in the waves.

So, we ask you: who are the true rulers of Earth?

Recently, you were witness to the drama played out in the presidential election crisis in the United States, headquarters of the Secret Government. Observe. These two very uncharismatic puppets, both funded by the same corporate giants, took not only the American nation but also the entire globe to the limits of frustration over who would be the "winner" and succeed in becoming the "most powerful man in the world."

You, who live within those borders, protested for these characters, pouring your energies into their insignificant debate, believing that one or the other should stand for your people ... just as much as you realized that neither had the brilliance nor the intention to effectively represent you. You went through the motions of casting your ballots, for this is the apex of your "democratic" process—yet you were shown (in the final analysis) that your votes do not count and that the process is completely corrupt!

All the while, the media and the manipulations of the puppeteers fuel separation amongst you, stimulating your loyalty to one or the other political party—while far greater concerns over your planet's ecological decline go unresolved and interest in true reform dies a most resounding death in the boardrooms of your so-called "World Leaders."

The campaign that establishes the global perspective of power has been designed so that all sentient beings of Planet Earth now perceive the Presidency of the United States as the absolute Throne of Power. This illusion has been created to prepare you for the One World Order, which, it **appears,** is being directed from that very seat. Yet, we remind you that those who are visible in the global arena (presidents, top government officials, and world leaders) are only figureheads. Their decisions are not their own: they are mere illusions—designed for you, the masses, by the strategists of the power elite.

However powerful they appear, remember that they are pawns in the hands of the master players ... decoys of the Secret Government. They act out their mandates, serving the Two Thousand, feeding the wealth and power-producing networks of dark design.

Those who slip through the nets by virtue of their impeccable commitment to justice and Truth—those who come in to truly represent humankind—are eliminated before they can complete their missions. You know who they are. You merely need to check the record, and you will find that most of the assassinated leaders in your history were, inevitably, working for global peace, equality, and the higher reflection of human potential.

We wish to suggest that the theater of the U.S. election in 2000 was constructed to foster your glorification of the democratic process and your belief in it, at a time when you are about to be herded into the cages of total domination. This event was staged as plans for the overt, global control of Planet Earth—the One World Order—reached completion.

It should be clear to you that it is the only true remaining superpower (the corporate-military complex directed from the United States) that openly dictates international policy, setting the terms of the global economy.

This, they tell you, is the spreading of "democracy" around the world.

And we cannot but ask you once again: who do you believe truly rules the Earth?

There are those of you who recognize how the strings of the power elite, who almost believe that they are the absolute rulers of the Earth realm, are being pulled by the highest levels of the Secret Government.

Others still believe the myth that it is the "elected" leaders who decide what goes there—in your world.

There are places where despots still cling to the illusion of power.

There still are tribal nations, where the mighty reign.

And there are priests and religious hierarchies, who claim to bring the word of the Ultimate down upon you, teaching you to fear God and repent your sins.

But these are not the true rulers of Earth, that magnificent orb which shines the hope of humanity through the Cosmos of Soul...

Will you rise up from your knees, never again to bow down before the lords of dark illusion?

Have you not humbled yourselves long enough?

Have you not sacrificed, served, and obeyed beyond the call of duty?

Children, will you stand for Truth from this day forward?

Listen.

In the final outcome, it is Gaia herself, great Celestial Being, who rules your world—you must never lose sight of the greater reality. Cosmic goddess, she is a unit of celestial consciousness, and she ultimately determines the outcome of all the life she bears. You, the most intelligent form of life there, are merely conscious units of Gaian biology, just as the cells and atoms of human essence are the elements of your personae.

If there is homage to be paid, then pay it to the Great Planet Earth. Go to the forests and the mountaintops and the oceans to celebrate her. Breathe in her wisdom, gaze upon her majesty, and feel the heartbeat of the Mother pulsing through your souls.

Sing her song.

Teach the children that they are her caretakers and that, by addressing the disharmony that has been for so long imposed upon the Earth, they, too, can help determine the outcome.

Encourage their concern, their awareness, and their awe. She will respond to that love, which will help calm the fury.

As we embark upon the unraveling of the secrets that have been woven into human societies (both ancient and new), we ask that you rediscover the true power that lies within you. We ask that you stand for Gaia, just as you must stand for every man, woman, and child who shares in her bounties.

Be empowered by what you will bring forward here, rather than to fear what might come from opening closed doors and looking down the deep, dark stairwells.

We feel that your success in clearing the dissonance of Gaia's fields depends largely upon your ability to deflect the controls of the Power, by reaching into the darkness of their misguided intentions and bringing the knowledge of their covert actions into the light—where all can be healed and forgiven.

We intend to help you achieve that.

It begins with your ability to hear, and then to see with your own eyes, the Truth that is being unearthed in these and other texts and all the wisdom that is being brought forward at this time of your liberation. We are confident that you have come to our teachings with open minds—else, how could we reach you? We ask that you spread the wisdom to others who may not yet have found the way but are searching for the path ... or a direction.

Let us deprive the dark rulers of their secrets by shining the laser-sharp light of knowledge into their coveted halls.

Let there be no more false masters.

6

Disarming the Dark Forces

So clever are the dark forces at manipulating your fear and survival instincts that they can deceive the majority (those who accept appearances for reality) at the conceptual level. They are expert stagehands, building scene after scene in the minds of the unsuspecting, who, in turn, become disempowered at the very idea of dark icons moving about in the material world and hovering in the ethers.

To the world of music, cinema, television, and the new electronic "realities," they bring overt and subliminal messages of the "evil" paradigm in every form, and children as well as elders shudder at the thought of somehow being clutched by the nightmare and destroyed.

Bear in mind, Dear Ones, that without "sinners" there would be no call for priests, without crime there would be no need for police, without your **obedience** there would be no way to **control** . . . and think, think, think about how that is put into place in your world.

Global news fills you with the horrifying and the grotesquely sensational, and always the demons of human cruelty and cult-like fanaticism fuel your misperceptions of a world leaning to the dark side.

The societal antidote, religion, carves out a way to salvation through the imposition of obedience, adherence to the dogma, and the threat of God's impending punishment to those who stray from the conventional doctrines of the church. This control system has been in place for countless millennia—from the time of the Last Generation of Atlantis, when the Power's experiment resulted in the sinking of the continent and, soon thereafter, the myth of avenging gods took hold in the earliest civilizations of the Sahara.

In every age, religious leaders hold sway over the minds, behavior, and lifestyles of the populace. It has been that way from the first human civilizations. Now, at the closing of the Age of Reason, organized religions are rallying, staking their renewed claim to your souls. They have paved the way of salvation, while their coffers spill over with the gold of your devotion and labor.

Know that the leaders of all religious empires—like all political figureheads—set the direction of their "spiritual" teachings according to the Power's mandates, for they, too, must follow the directives of the Secret Government. As the One World Order is put into place, they are preparing you for the One Religion—and that will not be Christianity, or Islam, or any other designated faith.

The One Religion of which we speak is the giving of yourselves totally to the idea that some "external" judge (whether that be your perception of a vindictive God or the Lords of the New Inquisition) punishes you for your sins and rewards your penance. This is the religion of Power: a way of controlling your actions and beliefs through spiritual reprisal (God's "wrath" upon you—the perennial sinners), and it is by far the darkest expression of their rule over you.

We suggest you take a closer look at those who insist that the way to heaven is upon the knees of obedience and that you walk, not crawl, along the path your soul designed when you first set out upon your exquisite journey.

The Christed One walked the Earth to show you the way out of blindness, and he was a rebel—a true anarchist. This, it seems, has been lost in the telling of his passing amongst you. He illuminated the path of true devotion, showing you the way within, where the godlight of Creation shines your own divinity. He personified forgiveness, compassion, and unconditional love. He healed the sick, taught the ignorant, and guided humankind into the light. He showed you that true religion—your connection to Prime Creator—is within you and that **love is the way and the glory.**

The Priesthood, aware of the disruptive impact the Christ's message would have had not only upon their immediate power but also the very future of organized religion, conspired—designing the stratagem of his assassination. They knew, as well, that they would have to rewrite history, so that the story of the Christ's appearance on Earth would paint a far different picture than that which had been etched upon the collective consciousness of that era. It would read Jesus Christ a martyr and glorify him as the selfless one who "died for your sins." It would empower the hierarchy with the care and keeping of the true records.

How is it that the existing Church of the Vengeful God managed to get away with murder of the Son while, simultaneously, convincing you of your indelible guilt? By casting blame upon the Roman overlord, Pontius Pilot, who agreed to the execution to appease the Priesthood, the Church walked away victorious—freed (on some levels) of the greatest anarchist to ever walk the Earth.

Know that appearances are not always what they seem, and so we ask you to think, Dear Ones ... rethink the myths and tales of human history.

You, the lightworkers of these times, are seeing beneath the surface, into the darkest depths of illusion, and by nature of that vision, you are beginning to neutralize the hold of the "phantom" over you, feeling liberated and aware.

That makes you prime targets, for, as awakeners of the race, your higher vibrations create significant disturbance in the control bands, where the masses are held immobilized in the lower frequencies by means of some particularly exotic technologies now being used against you by the Power—but these can be neutralized through right thought and action ... once the veil is lifted.

Don't think that your numbers have gone unnoticed or that your growing awareness of the covert management of Earth has somehow been deemed "insignificant" to the Secret Government. As the light of your knowledge and clear intention illuminate the way, the cloaked ones have had to develop strategies to deal with your brilliance, for you are upsetting their strategy of secrecy. Indeed, as you grow in numbers and in strength, giving voice to the silence of the ancients and the true story of human evolution, you are becoming enormously menacing to *The Plan*.

Embracing your newfound understanding of the intelligence

that permeates all existence, you feel the universal flame burning ever brighter and the power growing within and amongst you. Whereas before (a mere fifty years ago) your light was dim and scattered, it is now a glowing fire that cannot and will not be extinguished.

They simply had to come up with a strategy to deal with you, the "troublemakers" ... and they did.

Know that the best way to infiltrate your networks is by assuming the mannerisms, the appearance, and the language of the light teams. The darkest ones never dress of the black robe; you must know that by now. You must know that they would never reveal themselves so flagrantly—for they are most effective when they operate in shadow.

No, the systematic imprinting upon the unconscious of satanic icons, evil acts, and ghoulish images is intended for easier targets—the sleeping masses—for they are so bent in their fear that the mere conjuring of such images is enough to hold them in false worship—good "God-fearing" citizens, victims of their own ignorance.

You pose far greater challenges.

These troublesome characters (those we intend as the Power) do not expose themselves, parading around with skulls perched on scepters of evil, so do not let yourselves be activated in any way to hypnotically fear those archetypes. You will find them skulking about disguised as messengers of light, great political leaders, statesmen, intellectuals, priests, evangelists, and leaders of the spirit movement. They will feign that, like you, they are seekers of Truth, and they will attempt to deceive you every step of the way—for they are masters of illusion.

They are already well at work, infiltrating your light centers. That is why we feel compelled to bring this information full center, for your consideration and analysis. We believe that you must be far more discerning than ever before—no longer as eager children, grasping trustingly at all that is being made available to you ... but as wise seekers, who have learned that **there are also thorny stems where roses bloom.**

We have told you, at other moments of our teachings: it is important that you not blindly accept all information and individuals who have been positioned as bringers of enlightenment or social reform, for the ways of the dark side are elusive and you will simply have to have your eyes open ... your "sensors" fully operative. Question your sources. Hold them up to the light of your inner vision and be certain that what you perceive is not the inky reflection of watered-down truisms, but rather the sparkling clear ray of Truth, shining through.

There are gurus, those who stimulate you into renouncing your earthly possessions in the name of spiritual illumination, whose personal wealth is blatantly flaunted, garish and ostentatious, and still their mesmerized followers believe.

How is that?

One need only contemplate how a political leader can, in one breath, utter God's name in pious reverence, and in the next order the murder of the innocent in an act of war or punishment, never considering (or having to justify) how the two are totally irreconcilable. No one notices? It seems your nationalistic mantras of unity and might manage to override the public's need to question global military policies or the domestic violence that ravages the city streets.

Is there no contradiction there?

We are not suggesting that it is as simple to distract you, the awakening, for most of you see through the hypocrisy. Rather, we are warning you that the Secret Government knows that more sophisticated misinformation is going to be needed to deal with you, and it is currently being fed through your wires and into your networks. We are saying that you will be wise to scrutinize everything that comes into your consciousness more diligently...from this moment on...forever.

The quantity of deliberate misinformation that has already infiltrated your spiritual networks is enormous—and it is increasing dramatically. This ranges from the obvious to the sublime, whereby you are led to believe that you are really penetrating the impenetrable and gathering untold knowledge and wisdom from what are, instead, the coercive sources and intentionally misleading messages of the Power.

The time has come to devote care and integrity to your exchange of knowledge, filtering all that comes to you through your heart centers and then asking the inner voice to validate or discard whatever is meant to be held or released for your highest purpose.

What we recommend is that you utilize the mantra of sovereignty before entering into any experience, or space, or technology and then, once you have given the information its due respect, ask yourselves the vital question: does what you bring forth empower you, bringing joy, strength, and wonder, or does it evoke fear within you...feelings of helplessness and surrender?

At a time when, justifiably, much of your focus is becoming centered around conspiracy theories, it is important that you put any information that you are receiving to the test, for we are aware that they will utilize much trickery and illusion to steer you off course—not by openly censoring the messengers of the light (for you are far too many now and that would contradict the democracy paradigm).

A more far-reaching management tool is to simply create a deviation to your process—a deliberate misinformation network that will appear to be so totally revealing of the inner workings of the Secret Government and the individuals who comprise it that you will become inebriated by the sense of discovery and confirmation that will come from it. In short, you will embrace the planted information and spread its dark core material to others, becoming (in a most ingenuous way) a vehicle of the shadow.

As you pore through these tidbits of "inner circle" informants against the Government (here we speak of those who purport to be secret network infiltrators), you are to be stirred into feelings of hopelessness. You are to be seduced into believing that the plot against humankind is far more penetrating than you imagined and that the roots of darkness permeate far beyond your fields of operation and your ability to alter those realities. You are to believe that there is simply no way out of the downward spiral in which humankind **appears** to be eternally and irrevocably spinning out of control.

We are saying that if you come away from those sources overwhelmed by the information, feeling disempowered and stirred up in the lower vibrations of fear, survival, and sexuality... then you are not working with light-sourced information.

Be clear.

The Creator is everywhere around and within you, you are anchored to the Great Planet Earth, and Spirit is calling you ever upward. You came to climb higher, not to sink into the abyss.

You have heard the wake-up call, lightworkers of Gaia! Have you not yet shaken off your hypnotic slumber?

As the control mechanisms on Planet Earth intensify, the music of your celebration raises humanity from the tumult of fear and ignorance to lofty thoughts and a knowing... a remembering ... of why all of you have come.

The pursuit of knowledge and the acquisition of Truth feed your sanity; they ground and center you. The wisdom that is derived from that process fills you with fresh perspectives and ideas—the substance upon which human evolution thrives. However challenging, you are emboldened by what you are learning now, standing ever taller against the winds of change.

This is the path of all true seekers, and we commend you for your vision, your courage, and your conviction.

Your growing understanding of the structure of the One World Order is helping to dissolve it, freeing you to travel the path of the soul—upward, upon the magnificent spiral. The more you learn about their plan for the human race, the more resolute you become—and so much of what you once accepted and to which you resigned yourselves you are now beginning to question or reject entirely. Your eyes open, you recognize that the continuum of war, political crises, and domestic violence is not at all arbitrary, but that it is actually an underlying, progressive global campaign against the people of your world. You realize that globalization serves industry and the wealthy but de-humanizes the population. You see the irreparable damage the Earth suffers in the loath hands of your world leaders.

Dwindling numbers of human beings are still mesmerized by the fanfare and pageantry, for more and more of you are becoming intent upon listening to the music. As you recognize the rhythm, sense the pace, and observe the direction of the marching band, you divine where they are headed and when they will arrive. Such predictability, Dear Ones, creates a weak link in the chain of events they have planned for you—and it is there that you must concentrate your efforts.

There is, indeed, an "Order" to such process and, despite appearances, that is of great advantage to you—for you can work far more effectively with order than you can through chaos.

Once you recognize all the elements that contribute to the pattern, you will (by the very nature of consciousness) be altering it. Never forget that the mere observation of an experiment alters the outcome. In ways you may not understand, you will cause it to mutate and eventually self-destruct—for the design of the Secret Government never allowed for the possibility that such a multitude of rebel awakeners would rise up in this most crucial hour and stand for the human race. Nor did they imagine that you would ever reconnect with the Family of Light. They simply didn't expect to be "found out" because they never believed you capable of such insights.

Look at you. Do you acknowledge your own brilliance?

We do. We see the noble and compassionate aspects of your humanity—your capacity for remarkable achievement and the glory of your group soul. That is why you cannot help but realize that concealed in what can often appear to be "losing battles" are found enormous opportunities for the Spirit Self. You will see that by obstructing your will and attempting to manipulate you, the Power serves that purpose.

They, the bringers of the New World Order, are providing you with the quintessential test—the ultimate initiation—to become as adepts in the new realm of human experience or to sink into the confines of absolute limitation.

By scrambling to diffuse and silence you, they are linking you, conversely, to each other and giving you voice. Their dam of secrecy is breaking apart—splitting at the seams. First one, then another, and yet another hole in the dike breaks the silence, and they know they cannot hold back the rushing waters of your rebellion much longer. As they gather there, clutching at those crumbling walls, they have exposed to you the heel of Achilles.

Therefore, be discerning but fearless, remembering that the blossom of freedom takes seed in the fertile soil of your grounded awareness and blooms in the light of Truth. Claim your independence in every way, as sovereign beings, and spread a sense of integrity to all those you encounter. Above all, never lose sight of the fact that in the three-dimensional reality in which you reside, every aspect has its polar opposite—which is, at the same time, its complement . . . its mirror.

Therefore, if there is, indeed, such a commanding dark force working against you, there is (inherent in that duality) an equally powerful light force weaving a "New World Order" of its own: the Cosmic Unveiling.

We believe and have repeatedly stated that there is a great

awakening taking place in the Earth realm. We feel you stretching, the blood racing through your veins. We hear you breathing deeply, and we see with your eyes. We wish to help guide you all to put your thoughts, your emotions, and your resolve into even clearer focus ... so that the transformation will be made manifest in every part of your world—for the good of all humankind.

This has already begun.

We invite you, the awakeners, to look into the darkness with calm and circumspection, for **you must be fearless** in the wake of the changes that are washing over you. Fearing them, we remind you, fuels the dark intention. It brings you into resonance with it—which is why we are committed to helping you penetrate deep within their darkest caverns ... and your own deep, dark wells.

Your mere presence there will draw the light of love into those spaces. In ways you may not recognize, you will be healing them. You will find, in the end, that there is nothing there that you cannot identify and, acknowledging those beastly fears, you will indeed release them from your consciousness, so that you can get on with the work of raising Gaia.

That is what you came for ...

That is what you shall do.

7

One World Order

The One World Order—where the secrets and lies of those who have forever manipulated the human race are coming into full light—is upon you. We believe that this is becoming abundantly clear not only to those of you who lie directly in its path but to all who are even minimally aware of the tidal wave rushing over humanity... for the greatest storm of earth history is rising just beyond the confines of their locked doors and rose-covered garden walls.

All of you, in varying measure, will know its power, and through its dual nature—destructive and oppressive as it is cleansing and liberating—you will exercise your free will in determining just how you intend to weather the hurricane.

As frightening or disempowering as current world events may appear to you, remember that the all-out, belligerent attempt to take over Planet Earth is actually a much-needed catalyst that provides a majority of human beings a great opportunity to shake off the drug of indifference and stand for themselves and the greater society. Through their omniscient administration of the people of your world and their design to control every resource, those in power are openly obstructing liberty and blatantly defiling the planet. You simply can no longer pretend or be fooled into embracing the illusions of righteousness that they have projected into your fields of vision.

Great numbers of you are now seeing through the smokescreen—and that is a most positive aspect of this difficult time in your social evolution. And so we ask you to give great consideration and due contemplation to how the dark force is, in a very important sense, serving you ... for their tightening of the reins only stirs your desire and determination to run forever free—towards the light.

That, children, is **Justice** in its purest sense.

It is a most exquisite example of how light prevails. Let it serve as a lantern when the night of the Desert Days casts your mind into the shadowland that lies just over there—in the dark fields through which your star-lit path unwinds.

The architecture of their omnipotent design is crumbling, and so the pillars of power are wavering, soon to come down with a vengeance, as foreshadowed by the World Towers debacle. That cataclysmic event, the opening of the 11-11 portal, served as the trigger for the initiation of all those who will either be ascending with Gaia or going on to serve as lightworkers at their next station in the physical realm. So open your eyes, lightworkers all, to see opportunity rising from the dust and despair of destruction, and observe the outpouring of light into those obscure and ominous realms.

In truth, you have seen this coming. You have contributed to it in countless ways: as working members of your throwaway societies and as "drop outs"; as conscientious ecologists and as mindless consumers of Earth's resources; as thinking, concerned citizens of your troubled world and as oblivious passers-by. And so, we invite you not to gasp in despair at the magnitude of what appears to be overtaking your race or bury your heads in that hopelessness that has (momentarily) consumed so many souls on your planet, but rather to turn your acute attention to how this global tyranny is being imposed upon you, how you and the ones whose lives you affect co-create it … and **just what you can and what you intend to do about it.**

The continent of Europe has embarked upon the One Nation model of the United States of America, a collective of different customs, languages, and mores that are being homogenized into the one Europaland—where the Power intends that the traditions and the wisdom of the people be molded into a commonality that will simply not allow the ways of the ancients to survive, severing the cords of history and your ancestral connection to the Earth. This newly formed conglomerate will eventually unite more than forty-five nations under one currency, one trade policy, one military force, and one globalized consumer market.

Currently shifting into position under this great umbrella are the Eastern European nations, which (aided by the Soviet Union's fall from "superpower" status) are currently being drawn into the European community in the arms of the mechanism you identify as this "global economy." Russia—the crumbling remains of it—is still posed in the tenuous position of a "former" superpower, but as we communicate these transmissions you have already begun to see a realignment of that posture.

The positioning of Russia as a failed superpower, which served to enforce in your minds that communism had been all but stamped out and that what you have always feared as "the opposition" had been beaten into submission, will soon be bent into a new form—the sinewy shape of the awakening tiger and a cautious newcomer to the one overriding "democratic" force that polices the entire globe—or rather, a force intent upon "spreading democracy" as you are told by the leaders of these lands.

As mandated by the Secret Government, Britain stands apart—a great pillar unto itself, strictly aligned with the United States and a key player in the boardroom of the decision makers. Yet, it keeps one foot on the continent—ready to step in when added weight is needed there.

This new, centrally governed Europaland will be assimilated rapidly into the One World Order, whose operative nucleus lies in the Great Pentagon grid of the United States military and in the underground networks of the subsurface. There is where the real management of Earth takes place, and it is from there that the secretive rulers of your planet conduct their strategic business affairs.

China emerges as a mighty antagonist at this time, threatening on the one hand, trading on the other. This, too, is part of a greater global design, designed to keep you in survival mode, holding you to your belief that there is always a giant waiting to eat you, and always the great white father, your President, there to protect you.

Until the events of the imploding twin towers, the 11-11 gateway of humanity's explosive awakening, most of you believed the fairy tale. But the Twin Tower scenario tore away your illusions of safety...and that was deliberate. Now, as the totalitarian world government moves onto the grandstand, the Power needs to aggrandize your sleeping nemeses. They need to stimulate your ultimate fear now in order to justify the full-scale proliferation of a global military complex, fighters of all "evil" … everywhere in the world.

The Secret Government has reawakened the beast to convince you of your vulnerability, so that you will turn yourselves over completely and unquestioningly—while selling you on the need for such ridiculous schemes as the Space Wars Anti-Ballistic Missile System, which has (not at all mysteriously) reappeared at this time. You are being "terrorized" into believing in such inane orchestrations, as if shooting speeding nuclear warheads off their course from outer space might somehow save you from nuclear annihilation. As if the politics of war and destruction were as simple as a video game … where enemy ships streak across the screen, and they, the heroes, shoot them into oblivion.

As if there could be a "safe" place to hide on Planet Earth when those missiles start to fly.

Know that the awesome thermonuclear arsenals possessed by the top ten military nations are equipped with automatic response triggers. They are programmed with the precision of .00 seconds for launching in the event an enemy missile is deployed against you—all monitored via elaborate satellite networks in Earth's orbit.

As for the ceremonious passing of the infamous black box from one "Commander-in-Chief" to the next … be aware that the buttons are being pushed by powers far greater than those possessed by mere Presidents. The first nuclear missile to be fired will trigger an automatic, global nuclear holocaust and no "deterrent" is going to stop it once it is out of the box. Nothing can.

We suggest that all earth citizens for peace petition their governments to boycott the Star Wars Project and that citizens of the United States demand that funding from those trillion-dollar budgets be redirected towards resolving the more imminent nuclear threat on Planet Earth, which emanates from unstable and improperly manned nuclear reactors—since they are more than ready to blow.

∴∵∴

The positioning of China as the only true counter-power and the sudden emergence of rogue nations whose only purpose of existence is to destroy what is "good and just" in the world is being re-created in this phase of the attempted takeover of the entire human race to instill within you absolute polar consciousness. It is designed to glorify, in a "might makes right" context, how the democracy ideal—"goodness"—triumphs over all. From that reference point, the so-called "free world" leaders intend to eradicate once and forever all enemies of what you are to believe is the Global Democratic Alliance—imposing their ethics in every capital of the world, in every village and every town.

Then, Dear Ones, you will be left with only the so-called "democratic" government—the One World Order—to rule over you.

You, the people of the righteous alliance, are being misled with all of this nonsense—still playing cowboys and Indians, still believing in the good guy/bad guy political arena. When are you, as a global society, going to understand that the theater of war is merely a distraction?

It is you that they are fighting: you, the human race, are the target of the Secret Government—**you** are the "Indians."

Be wary of the "right way" paradigm, for your believing it is part of your social programming, driving you headfirst into the One World Order, where there would be the "only" way. Were you to be caught in that cage, it would be far more difficult to recognize how you had been corralled into those fences with such illusions and then maneuvered into position.

You see that in order to create the model of the "right" side, there has to exist an opposition force that is, somehow, "evil" in its fundamental reasoning—because to be "right" in polarized thinking means to be inherently "good." The communist sees capitalism as you see that socioeconomic system—the root of all social decline; (s)he sees the same goodness in that system as you see in yours—for this is what inspires your dedication to a belief, and it is what determines your adherence to a principle.

What neither part recognizes is that each is the polar reflection of the other and that the dynamic tension created by that duality only fortifies the overriding force—the Authority! Each is necessary to the other, for the foundation of any dogmatic credo is the belief in the existence of an opposing doctrine that would have, as an objective, the elimination of the other . . . hence, those who ask you to kill, fight, or finance your nation must continually nourish your conviction that yours is the right way and that any other system is wrong.

Also involved in the process of stimulating your patriotic allegiance is the exaltation of the belief that the "wrong way" nations are set upon your destruction. Therein lies the dynamic that defines polarity consciousness, as it is currently being played out on global planes.

It is the agent that binds the political soup in which you are currently swimming.

The power elite know how you resist overtly dark masters, and they do recognize how blatantly enslaving you renders you uncontrollable and unproductive. They have attempted it—time and time again—only to find that you eventually rebel against the whip and cage. They have learned that it is a far more effective management strategy to create within you the illusion that you are the drivers of your society. This, in their eyes, is the global solution.

First, they had to create the archetypal, invincible nation—an overriding authority to emerge from what you refer to as World War II. The United States, positioned as the champion of freedom and fighter of tyranny, stepped victoriously onto the winner's podium and took the gold, in every manner of speaking. England took silver. Russia **was given** the bronze—and soon after it was taken away.

As citizens of the "free" world, you have been led to believe that all other systems are inferior to yours and that the world will be a better place when, everywhere, your ethics have been imposed (denying, of course, freedom to those who are forced to embrace your system). You are far more manageable when you feel righteous and believe the justifications and excuses you are given for your nations' aggressions and misdeeds.

By "breaking" the Soviet Union, the orchestrators of earth politics have reinforced within you the illusion that their "good" always triumphs over "evil" and that you, citizens of democratic nations, are on the right side of that perennial battle between the dark and light forces—justifying even such unthinkable acts as the dropping of nuclear warheads upon the human beings and the animal and plant kingdoms of Japan.

Bear in mind that such political posturing and the resulting wars and perennial violence are all part of a quite specific process in which the western world is being brainwashed into accepting that only a central government will be able to police the world, prevent global destruction, hold the economy, and preserve whatever quality of life you live from being stolen out from under.

They are certain of your acquiescence, for they have put so much of their dark plan into place in so little time and you, the race, have stood by, watching. You have allowed it. Indeed, you have fueled and served them in the past and the mass of humanity still does. And it is so that we hasten you, the awakening, to move into the action zone, applying all of your wisdom and knowledge—the concentration of mind, heart, and soul—to alter their process.

Large areas of the continent of Africa, exploited since the very first waves of Annunaki explorers came into earth space, have been stripped of most of their mineral wealth and resources—although there are still fortunes to be extracted at key locations there. Parts of the continent of Africa are barren and unyielding, others are being poisoned by the ravages of civil war, and all is being left to wither and die—for there is not that much left to take from those lands.

In truth, deep Africa is viewed by the Power as the collective waste station of Planet Earth.

As for human lives and the wealth of animal and plant species still struggling to survive upon that continent ... surely you recognize the token efforts being undertaken by your United Nations organizations as little more than political anodyne for the suffering there. Despite the gestures of aid for Africa, being touted as the humanitarian efforts of your global governments, almost nothing is being done to save the dying and prevent the killing in these abandoned worlds.

We remind you, too, that Black Africa has long been a test tube for the refinement of laboratory-created super viruses: those that are known to you, such as Ebola and AIDS, and others, such as the West Nile virus, that are only now beginning to surface. For the Power it is, above all, a primary market for the sale of second-hand weapons and war machinery, and so it provides them a twofold solution: first, it serves as a thriving arms and ammunition market for the massive dumping of weapons; second, political interests there continue to create great killing fields of innocents, helping to cull the population.

In essence, they are acting out a most perverse war game. The tribal conflicts of Africa—the massacres and civilian shootings—have the people of those regions doing the Secret Government's dirtiest work. Not only does the ceaseless killing help to eradicate an "expendable" population but the puppet governments there even pay the Authority for the privilege of killing and destroying their own people.

It is the same for much of India and its neighbors, lands of unimaginable poverty, overpopulation, and disease. There are, however, deep pockets of much sought-after uranium, which hold the Secret Government's fascination, and (as you have been made acutely aware) there are nuclear arsenals in those territories. As the plan to put a global military command into place takes form, India has become a strategic location for the Power and will soon be targeted for surrender to their authority or takeover by the administrators of "justice."

The great island continent of Australia is also uranium-rich, and this is of great significance to the warring world. Once an isolated and sacred land, Australia has now been fully integrated into the global economy and policy setting of the New Order.

Oil-producing nations of the Middle East, as you well know, still hold center stage due to their abundance of petroleum (sucked from the earth and siphoned into the coffers of the power elite) and, moreover, due to the opportunities that are created there for the staging of wars, political crises, and global "tension." The electromagnetic grid is at its most intense in this part of your world. This has everything to do with why the Christ chose this location when he appeared in your dimension and why the Great Pyramid was placed in its strategic geometrical location in the region.

For strategic economic and political reasons, the Middle East has been designed to be a hotbed of violence, and they intend that it so remain. As for the current crises in those regions, all created by the Power from the lust for more wealth and control over the global population, just remember ... if there are no enemies threatening not only the physical borders but also your philosophical boundaries, how will the Power justify to you the ungodly sums of capital—your tax tithings—that they are determined to invest and disguise as military spending, intelligence gathering, and the technologies of global control?

There are, of course, other interests in other lands, for (besides the exploitation of Earth's minerals) substantial wealth is derived from the proliferation and distribution of illegal drugs worldwide.

Consider what is required to extract an ounce of gold from the deep earth and know that the same amount of pure heroin (derived from opium), which grows as weed in Asian and South American fields, is worth tenfold the precious ore in the marketplace. Those countries that are heavily indebted to the western nations must repay their high-interest loans, and from where do you imagine that revenue will come? Do you really believe that, despite your awesome military capabilities and stockpiles of toxic chemical agents, your governments cannot manage to wipe the weed, once and forever, from the face of the Earth?

By now you must realize that drug trafficking and the addiction of so many human beings is a planned phenomenon—a strategic marketing ploy—created not only for the wealth that it provides the commanders and their masters.

Weeds, Dear Ones, are far more easily harvested than ores and the liquid gold of the oil fields, and you cannot begin to imagine the wealth that is derived from this industry. Consider, too, how the drug phenomenon has, in the relatively brief time of its global proliferation, served to alienate, disempower, and control millions upon millions of users around the globe . . . and remember that **control is the primary objective of the One World Order.**

In case it has not yet come clear in your minds, we are telling you that the Secret Government intends to use whatever means necessary to impose no less than a totalitarian state from Alaska to Zanzibar. They envision a borderless world where every aspect of your lives would be openly determined by a Central Power— a world where freedom of thought and action would be annihilated forever ... supplanted by absolute obedience on mental, emotional, and physical levels. A world in which rebellion could no longer take seed.

Fortunately, this despotic scenario cannot play out, for the events now unfolding in earth reality, orchestrated by the celestial deities as well as human consciousness, are simply leading *Homo sapiens* in another direction.

Despite the immensity of the shadow, more light surrounds your world than does the darkness penetrate there.

The imminent ascension of Gaia—so close you can already feel yourselves spinning—denies the successful imposition of these and other mechanisms of destruction, and you possess untold faculties from which to build your personal and communal processes—your approach—to the unfolding of these, the Desert Days of Planet Earth.

8

Drugs and Arms:
The Lies You Have Been Sold

The two most profitable industries of Earth are drug trafficking (both illicit and legal) and the arms trade. Their proliferation is fruit of the Authority's unquenchable thirst for wealth, power, and control over your individual lives and upon the global society ... and it is time you realize how and why these plagues have been brought down upon the human race and what you can do to reverse their proliferation in the global society.

The truth regarding their diffusion in your world is far different than the story and the lies that are being fed to you. It results from complex mechanisms that were set in motion many thousands of years ago, evolving over the millennia into an all-out campaign against the whole of humanity—as it is manifesting through the One World Order for global domination.

By stimulating the lower aspects of human behavior through arousal of the "animal" self, those who have ruled over the human race have maneuvered you into societal structures that provide consumers as well as financiers for all their dirty doings—a world in which the "haves" and the "have-nots" battle it out against each other to claim their very small piece of the ever-elusive pie in the sky.

Just moments after your infancy as a race, you were ripped from the embrace of the Earth Mother and corralled into the labor camps of the first earth societies, where you have remained ever since. From the time of your earliest history, you have been harnessed to serve the Power. You have spent your lives competing one against the other, while creating extraordinary wealth for the elite. You have fought wars for them, convinced of the need, the might, and the right of the masters. You have embraced and become addicted to their drugs ... you have accepted their relentless media exploitation of your "animal" selves. You have poisoned the earth, the sea, and the sky with your unnecessary waste and their short-term vision.

It has been a sobering thing to behold—especially knowing what we do of your birthright and the legacy of *Homo sapiens*.

For centuries, you have been taught that the enslavement of your species bears the greasy imprint of human hands—cast upon the collective unconscious of Gaia. But when one holds the story up to the light, the brand of the dark warriors clearly appears, seared into the rich fiber of human history.

We believe it is time you recognized the signet of those who secretly claim ownership of the people of Earth, for the more you expose that stain to the radiance, the quicker it will fade away ... just as pain is silenced when it lets go to healing.

Will you join us in holding the earth chronicles up against the light of Ra?

The Drug Trade

We have briefly shared our ideas regarding the true nature of international drug trafficking, but it is important that we enlarge our field of vision to include the far greater drug problem plaguing your more affluent societies.

The taking of addictive drugs is, in every way, a detriment to your well-being and the soul's journey, and there is no question that harmonious, balanced individuals do not consciously inject deadly poisons and addictions into their bodies ... **is there?**

It is madness—a form of self-loathing and destruction—and it is difficult for most of you to imagine such aberrant behavior. Yet, as you observe the state of civil affairs through the drone of your mainstream media and your own observations of street life in the cities and towns where you live, you cannot deny that growing numbers of individuals are doing just that—allowing themselves to be captured and sucked downward, trapped in the helix of darkness.

There are those who do consciously bow down to the dark masters—who are then cast off as the "dregs" of society, considered the deviates of your otherwise "wholesome" communities. It seems that such alienating perceptions are comforting to those who do not suffer from such destructive addictions, as if they somehow remove them from the drug problem and its implication for the greater society. As if it could never happen to them or to their loved ones. As if it simply isn't part of their world, but it is ... isn't it?

Drug trafficking and the substance addiction and dependencies it generates are not limited to the world of pushers and backstreets and alleys—of degenerates and misfits. Alongside illicit drug dealing and its deep penetration into every level of your global society exists a parallel drug trade, which consists of a vast assortment of highly priced pharmaceutical drugs (those sold by respectable, establishment druggists) and an enormous multinational public that forms an inexhaustible clientele. Directly involved in the trade are reputable establishment doctors, whose medical training has been designed to teach them to overmedicate the population with powerful (and unnecessary) chemicals ... and patients, who blindly accept their diagnoses and prescriptions.

Far too many human beings consistently ingest chemicals without thinking, and the industry thrives—fortunes are made— from their believing themselves ill or from self-medicating to anesthetize and suppress all pain, negative emotions, and surfacing symptoms. We wonder when they will recognize how, with the proliferation of every imaginable kind of quick-fix remedy, human malaise is perpetuated.

If you examine the situation, you cannot but realize that, despite all your technological advances and medical breakthroughs, those of the industrialized nations do seem to be living longer ... but in declining states of mental, physical, and spiritual health.

Those who are apt to point fingers and condemn drug-users, while filling their medicine cabinets with a range of over-the-counter pharmaceuticals that define your "socially approved" remedies, would be wise to reconsider the meaning of "drug abuse." Simply because they do not partake of illegal opiates from the corner dealer does not mean they are of the un-hooked generation.

You, the awakening, are spreading the word—revitalizing human knowledge of mind over matter and an understanding of the fountain of energy that surges forth from every living entity. As poles of the establishment, you have your work cut out for you! To be credible and persuasive—to really effect change—it will be necessary that you serve as models of integrity, happiness, and good health.

You will have to "do the work" on yourselves before you can effectively serve others in this capacity.

Know that the all-pervasive pharmaceutical industry, with its multibillion-dollar lobby of world politicians, depends upon three basic marketing paradigms for its continued success in the legalized drugging of your world populations.

The first is that individuals of your contemporary "westernized" societies (the archetypal capitalistic nations) tend to give their power away to easy solutions and quick-fix remedies, rather than to explore the entirety (the cause and effect of their actions) and so heal their lives, creating perennial well-being of mind, body, and soul. Within this fundamental social context, they can entrain and market you to believe that, with the first sniffle or pain, you must run to the nearest pharmacy and fill yourselves with "incredibly fast relief" from all that ails you.

The second is that the increasingly toxic environment, poisonous food supply, and negative entrainment from your media provide the fundamental parameters of "dis-ease" within you, promoting unwellness in growing numbers of the population, so that there is an unlimited and escalating market available to them. Bear in mind that if you begin to believe that you are well and then create and manifest that harmony within your bodies, you will no longer require their big-profit remedies for your perpetual ailments.

We are telling you that the pharmaceutical corporations, "regulated" by the Food and Drug Administration and its global counterparts, are interested not in making you well but in locking you into states of perpetual disharmony and chronic illness. Indeed, these regulating bodies are created at the governmental level to protect and foster the hugely profitable pharmaceutical industry, while all along you think they are working for you … don't you? You must understand that without your "disease," a collective hypochondria, and your belief in the body's ability to process out the symptomatic fluctuations of its fight against illness, the "chemists" have no market.

Your good health, sweet children, is simply not good business.

Do you see how much of your collective "dis-ease" and pain is nurtured and stimulated at the societal level, to assure that you will buy the "immediate relief" formulas and, in so doing, remain dependent upon the need for their drugs?

We understand that to be addiction. Do you?

It should not surprise you that alternative health methods, such as the use of plant essences and the laying on of hands, are ridiculed and distrusted by the mainstream. Indeed, we observe how the industry is attempting to shut you down, to stamp out all grassroots movements that offer alternatives and choice—to prohibit you from overseeing your own mind/body well-being. Consider: if you, as an entirety, realize that you can create and maintain excellent health on your own—without their drugs—what will that mean to their profit lines?

The third marketing principal of the pharmaceutical industry, then, is that a sick society is a profitable society … so where does that leave you? If you still believe that a multibillion-dollar industry that thrives upon your illness has, as its objective, the curing of disease and unwellness, then you are far more gullible than you think.

We believe that the legal sale of pharmaceutical drugs poses a far greater danger to human beings than the illegal drug trade, for the commercialization and government approval of such legitimate drugs lulls most of the race into believing that they are "good" for you and that you need them to maintain your health and to suffer not even one minute of discomfort.

Open your medicine cabinets. Examine your household stockades of pharmaceuticals. Do you really need these chemical concoctions, of which you know so very little? What are you actually putting into your systems when you inject their deadly vaccines and swallow the pills and syrups that promise to bring relief of your temporary ailments?

Although the increasingly toxic environments of Earth pose far greater challenges than ever before, the human body (nourished through a balanced approach to eating, a healthy environment, and a positive mental outlook) does not require chemicals to keep a healthy balance. Enough of you are well aware of the importance of establishing a balanced diet, of exercising, and of getting enough rest that we need not elaborate those fundamentals here. What is important to our discussion is your use of medication as a way of overriding symptoms of disharmony in the body—symptoms that must be identified as indicators of the physical condition and then duly treated with consideration of the entire organism.

If you suffer from a headache, it is a short-sighted solution to turn immediately to chemicals that remove the pain—chemicals that create long-term side-effects in the body. Aspirin, for example, causes stomach bleeding—this is a known effect of aspirin usage. Yet, you continue to consume untold quantities of it, as if headache discomfort were a far greater ill than internal bleeding.

Know that side effects are built into most medications, so that you will graduate, in a sense, from the immediate relief remedies to yet other chemicals for suppression of secondary symptoms.

It is, indeed, a conspiracy against you.

Every kind of pill is available for headache pain, muscle discomfort, colds and flu, indigestion, nervousness, and lethargy. Yet, all of these are symptoms of some aspect of imbalance within you that must be approached at the causal level—rather than masking the symptoms. There are medications to anesthetize you, to energize you, to cool you down, to heat you up. There are pills to clear your brains and pills to fog them over ... these are proliferating as the emotional depression of your youth and adult populations reaches pandemic proportions.

Of the dangers of antidepressant medications, there is so much you do not know—yet they are widely prescribed as the remedy to emotional pain, and far too many of you accept them. They are the ultimate statement of your inability, as a society and as individuals, to cope with the emotional malaise of your generations.

You are not chemists. Those who are, however, know what possible side effects such powerful concoctions have on the human nervous and endocrine systems. We dare state that some of these have been deliberately built into the drugs, for reasons that involve mind control of certain factions of the society. After all, what better way to break down your resistance to authority than by drugging you into unreal states of altered consciousness … dulling your perceptions of reality and your own identities?

The list of antidepressant medications is growing as your collective mental health declines, yet still you do not recognize the enormous profit that is derived from your mental disorientation and physical illness—or the mere symptoms of "dis-ease." If you are sick, unhappy, or feeling emotionally unstable, it is a reflection of negative factors in your lives that must be dealt with or removed, which allows the body and mind to reestablish good health and the radiance of Spirit.

Unfortunately, rather than getting to the source of those dark sentiments that cloud over human ability to cope with life, far too many doctors medicate to anesthetize the emotional pain—deactivating the pleasure sensations as well. With time, one learns to feel nothing at all—neither pain nor joy—and that is a highly interesting prospect for those who wish to dominate you and control your thoughts and habits.

So many robots now walk your neighborhoods, their minds altered from antidepressants and mood-altering medications. They are respectable people, pillars of the society—closet addicts. And what of the children? We observe how your troubled youth, depressed over the state of your world and the outlook for their own survival, are being systematically placed on highly dangerous medications—numbed into believing that they are somehow "managing" their depression.

Growing numbers of these individuals have been stripped of the ability to feel anything at all; you must question whether this is a viable alternative to the pain of dark emotion—however filled with despair. You must ask yourselves how these adults of the tomorrow are going to cope with the difficulties that you are confronting now and with others that lie just ahead of you.

It is as if the society, as a whole, refuses to confront its growing desperation, for then the entire human race will have to deal with the very real questions that you, the awakeners, are now facing **head on.** Most are too anesthetized or distracted, and without a truly spiritual understanding of evolution and the death process, it is simply too frightening.

The numbing of your bodies, minds, and souls is not only an ineffective approach to healing—it is an act of renouncing your freedom to become fully conscious human beings. We call upon you, the awakeners, to refuse these drugs and to lead a campaign against them. We remind you that you are the masters of your own destinies, and with your growing understanding of the forces at work in your world you have a clear responsibility to yourselves and to the society-at-large to reject the imposition of their opiates and walk in the glow of good health and peace of mind.

Remember . . . you were born to greatness—free-will beings of the infinite Universe. Sparks of godlight, you are unlimited and you are brilliant—a super race of beings. Only fear and ignorance can drag you down into the bottomless pits of your imagination . . . and so remember to shine the light into the deepest chasms. There you will see that even from the cold, dark blackness can emerge new and inviting landscapes.

Lessons will be learned from those visions.

Be brave and defiant, for you are sovereign—the curators of

your own well-being and the guardians of Gaia. We call upon you to release yourselves from every form (mental and physical) of drug addiction, taking back whatever you have given away to the Power and giving back to the Goddess whatever you have taken from the Earth.

Once you are absolute in your clarity and resolve, you can assist others in the process. This is the purest expression of your intent to bring to full integrity the body, mind, and soul.

What can be done?

- Commit, as a first step, to drastically reducing the amount of television input and other forms of publicity that destroy your peace of mind and plant the hypnotic suggestion to medicate. Parents and guardians can help the children by restricting access to violent programming and interactive video games, where they are being entrained with psychotic behaviors and scripted with the killing instinct.

- Examine all pharmaceuticals (particularly over-the-counter remedies) in your medicine chests: read every label, study the contents, and then ask yourselves if you can do without them—eliminating whatever you can.

- Read labels. These invasive chemicals are harmful and usually unnecessary. They mask what is causing the imbalance in your being. Although you cannot be expected to know the chemical terminology of the ingredients, study the "possible side effects" that are indicated in the information provided with the drug—what is being introduced into your bodies?

- Be aware that you can be easily entrained by the ailments of others and commit to being well—demand it of your bodies.

Talk about feeling well, live the radiance of good health, and shine it out to others. Your luminous reflection will help heal the world.

- Eliminate, as much as you can, all synthetic foodstuffs and vitamins, as they create disharmony in your bodies. If you must take a vitamin supplement, see that it is an organic compound. Better still, develop a food regime whereby vitamins, nutrients, and enzymes are brought into your being directly from the natural food source.

- Consider alternative health methods and the holistic approach to well-being. All-too-often, you reach for the remedy before you have allowed the body to process out the "dis-ease." It is important to understand the source of any pain or discomfort; often, its manifestation is the body's way of expressing the cause, and you must listen... you must experience the temporary symptom so that you can get to the source.

- Investigate massage therapies, yoga, pranic healing, and go to green pastures, listen to birdsong, breathe country air... plant flowers everywhere around you.

- When you are tired, rest. If you have a cold or flu virus, it will have to run its course, and no medication yet exists on Earth that can prevent it—nor will it ever, for your obsessive masking of cold and flu symptoms forms one of the most profitable baselines of the pharmaceutical empire. In many cases, the temporary upset is your body's way of getting you to lie down and turn off the mental machinery that drives you into states of extreme fatigue and illness. Therefore, rather than fill yourselves with every kind of syrup, decongestant, and antibiotic medication, stay warm, sleep, and take comfort in rest. You will see that it will pass, and you will be, in some subtle ways, the better for it.

- If you are nervous and irritable, it is a sign that your life is out of balance. Rather than numb yourselves with sedation or antidepressant medication, journey within to find the true cause of the irritation. You will find you need more play in your lives ... more fun ... more movement. Get outdoors ... to the trees and the oceans and breathe in Mother Nature. This is all the more valid for the children, who are being medicated **unnecessarily** and with ominous implications for their mental, physical, and spiritual well-being.

- Eliminate, as much as you can, poisons in your system: excessive amounts of coffee, tea, alcohol, sugar, nicotine, food additives, and all chemical compounds that disturb the natural balance.

- **Test your pain levels.** You will find that you can, indeed, tolerate minor headaches and discomfort and that they do often pass on their own.

- Question your doctors: you should know exactly what it is they are prescribing before you agree to ingest it. And remember that most of them have been trained to **treat the symptoms** rather than the cause, as they have been marketed to medicate rather than heal.

The Arms Race

Just as you are made to believe you are sick so that you will obsessively and compulsively medicate, so are you sold to believe in a perennially menacing enemy, so that you will finance the broadscale trafficking of mass weapons of destruction, war machinery, and arms of every imaginable form and dimension.

Were you to take the time to do a bit of global accounting and actually investigate the military budgets of even just the industrialized nations, you would be sure to feel your collective jaws hitting the proverbial table. Imagine, then, the entire trade— the secret military agendas and illegal arms traffic worldwide as well as the runaway arms race at home. Rest assured that the profound wealth derived from weapons and war is so astronomical that you, individuals of the planet, simply cannot fathom such figures ... nor can you begin to imagine just how vast are the arsenals of destruction that currently exist on Planet Earth.

Yet, paradoxically, **you finance war,** and by financing it, you indirectly encourage the violent solution—although we are not suggesting that you are necessarily violent individuals. Rather, it is your cultivated apathy and alienation from government that allows your leaders to push through their military budgets and sell you, the people of Earth, the distorted idea that military might is the way to peace.

To sell this concept to the "civilized" society, there must be enemies to fight and borders to protect. There must be a right way ("yours") and everything else ("theirs"). With time, this stereotype of justice filters down to the individual level, and you begin to believe that violence is the only solution. Justified by the role models set by your governments, you buy guns to take what is not yours or to protect what is. Add to this toxic cocktail the glorification of violence in your media, your "toys" and entertainment, and the use of drugs to dull the pain, sedate, and mask the symptoms of mental and emotional imbalance ... and lo and behold! Suddenly you find you are living in a violent, dysfunctional society.

Observing the state of your world, you can only surmise that such an approach is a dismal failure.

Face it. War and weapons are big business, and ironically you—seekers of peace and happiness—are the financiers. This is only one of many examples of how the dark forces manipulate you into serving their interests, and you need to consider this aspect, despite your conscious conviction that you are working for the light and light alone.

Besides being taxed into financing war, your societies provide armies of their youth to do the dirty work of fighting, killing, and dying in those wars. Processed through rigid military training camps, they are brutalized into becoming kill-enabling mechanisms of war—indoctrinated with the fervor of patriotic allegiance, desensitized by the brutality of their training, and conditioned into military obedience. There, say officials, they learn "discipline and responsibility," but what is really happening in the boot camps is that your young men and women are being prepared to kill or be killed in the fields of senseless death and destruction.

These are your brothers, husbands, daughters, and sons, and they are being trained to kill, upon order, the brothers, husbands, daughters, and sons of "enemy" men, women, and children.

Somehow, the fact that they are trained as the **legalized killers** of your nations seems to make the outright murder of "the enemy" strangely heroic—yet you cringe at the idea of murder and violence within your fences.

How does the "civilized" society reconcile such a dichotomy?

It is not our purpose here to elaborate the nature of violence, for that is a subject that would require far greater detail and concentration than we can provide in this particular text. Our concern is that you understand how you are marketed and sold on the necessity for the violent solution on various levels ... and how you are then indoctrinated into fighting other people's wars, financing and perpetuating them.

We ask you to consider that this evil is not rooted in ideology—the merit of one belief structure over another. It is not about opposing religions—the intolerance of others in the name of the One and Only God. Nor is it an act of justice, or humanity, or the forced resolution to irreconcilable political conflict.

War is an economic necessity for the producers of weapons of mass destruction and military machinery—regulated by the industrialized nations. Within the hallowed halls of the governmental committees and world leaders, they are trading fast and furiously ... a veritable shark frenzy. Just as they design drugs to keep you sick, so do they create wars to sell arms. The stories and threats that are sold to you as justification are illusion—dark shadows that shroud human ability to recognize its demons.

Although within your United Nations framework one does find truly dedicated workers for peace, it is, by-and-large, a façade. By nature of the financial gains from the proliferation of arms, that Council's role is to serve (in appearance) as arbitrator of global tension and political unrest.

The governments that finance the United Nations and their military leaders have a vested interest in armed conflict and we observe that the forces of military aggression are dedicated to war—for without it, they have no reason to exist. There can be no hierarchy, no five-star generals, no trillion-dollar budgets, and no war games without war or the menace of it.

Consider the Yugoslavian crisis of some years past. As your world leaders sat idly by, you—citizens of the world—watched the massacre of the innocent become the top story of every news network ... in every country. You became, in a very short time, anesthetized to that violence, for it was so emotionally exploiting and incessant that you, the viewers of crude brutality, had to become desensitized to such savage cruelty in order to cope with it. In time, we observed, your horror turned to "boredom," and the broadcasters, aware they were losing their ratings, moved that bubbling cauldron—the blood of Yugoslavia—onto the back burner.

Behind the scenes, the "democratic" nations (self-declared "peacekeepers") as well as the mirror nations were selling both sides their "cast-off" arms, ammunition, and military supplies. Fortunes were amassed by private interests, as well as governments ... and it was only upon reaching market saturation that the conflagration wound down and a form of resolution was achieved.

Were it not for the many great humanitarians (mostly those working from behind the scenes) dedicated to the pursuit of peace and the betterment of the human condition, you might very well have blown yourselves to bits centuries ago ... so determined are they to bury your world in mortar and shell.

And what of the war on your city streets—there where it is "illegal" to kill the other? You have witnessed how a totalitarian state that aspires to controlling the population allows no citizen (other than the indoctrinated militia) to possess arms. Feeling no need for pretense or concealment, the dictatorial government imposes martial law upon the people for the obvious purpose of creating a sense of fear of the ruling order, demanding obedience and suppressing all thoughts of rebellion.

You, of the archetypal "democratic" nation, the United States, have (until now) enjoyed the right to carry and bear arms, as it was written in the Constitution of your nation by men who recognized the potential for tyranny in the New World—themselves rebels against the absolute power of the ruling monarchy. But now, when violence from guns and other attack weapons has become endemic in your society, you are being pushed towards a renewed prohibition, where no citizen will be allowed to purchase or own firearms.

It would mean a loss of substantial revenue for the government, but your leaders have weighed that against the value of your policed obedience, and there is simply no contest. The campaign began long ago, and you are now being maneuvered into position, entrained by media sensationalism and political rhetoric to lay down your arms.

To law-abiding individuals this makes sense, and you welcome this concept—the outlawing of firearms—for it sounds like the only solution to the crises in your neighborhoods and big cities. But consider this:

> **"When guns are outlawed, only . . .**
> *the National Security Agency*
> *the Secret Service,*
> *the military,*
> *the FBI,*
> *the CIA,*
> *Interpol,*

the state police,
the local police,
the Highway Patrol,
the National Guard,
bank guards,
private investigators,
the 'peacekeeping forces' and
***outlaws will have guns.* "**

We believe weapons and the warring mind to be the undoing of all civilizations, and our wish for the people of Earth is that you could enjoy a world without war and violence and simply live in peace. Unfortunately, that is not the present reality upon most of your planet, for you are bound in the tether of such intense polar opposition that disharmony seeps into every level.

The question that you must contemplate now is this: what would happen were the Secret Government to decide that the time has come to impose martial law . . . first in America, then in the rest of the world?

Those in leadership roles now are preparing the way, filling you with new fears of unseen enemies—both domestic and foreign—calling you to their churches, trumping up your patriotic zeal, and exalting your sense of righteousness over "the other." While torturing and murdering "the enemy," they are capitalizing upon the proliferation of violence in your cities to maneuver you into accepting the outlawing of guns—it is imminent—and we invite you to exercise your keenest abilities of observation when examining the deep implications of that process.

We are not calling you take arms against your government

(**as it did** with the people of Yugoslavia, inciting them to take down the dictator). We believe that right thought, right speech, and right action must form the structure of your conscious rebellion, and that you must raise the voice of your protest through your unity and sheer numbers—not with weaponry and violence. But we do wish to remind you that the Great Democracy of America was designed by the founding forefathers with many checks and balances, so that tyranny could never take hold.

Your right to bear arms was written into your constitution to hold the government to its word. Therefore, think it through carefully before you vote it out, since the Power will interpret such a collective statement as your absolute resignation.

A lot more than just the wisdom of those you revere as the wise founders of your nation may hang on such decisions.

9

Hidden Cameras and Secret Weapons in Space

We have suggested that the Secret Government's space agenda is not at all what it seems, and we have told you, in earlier transmissions, about the colony that is already bustling about on the Moon. The NASA Division now reports discovery of water there, as well as upon Mars and other celestial bodies in your solar system—these are observations that we brought to you in the first book of the trilogy, and we observe that the elements required to colonize the Moon and Mars are now being openly elaborated by the scientists.

Since bringing you that information years ago, much has appeared from your scientific community to support our claims and what may have seemed like fiction then is now sounding terribly **scientific** just a very few years later.

Things are, indeed, speeding up in your quadrant of the galaxy.

You are being fed a wealth of selected and screened information regarding the discoveries that are far from new in the neighborhoods of your celestial family, so that your global corporate/military complex can take its enormous leaps into space without question or scrutiny. The military overlords have received direction from the Government to manage the earth crisis from that vantage point, while preparing the way of their impending evacuation.

Few of you are paying much attention to their findings.

As always, you, the people, are the financiers of the Power's tinkering about in space, but you are only beginning to gain awareness of the true nature of the space program, and the human race, on the whole, doesn't particularly care—yet.

Not until you are openly contacted by alien civilizations will the whole of earth society begin to look feverishly outward, to space, finally realizing how that which your leaders are projecting out past earth orbit has everything to do with what is being called back in to you.

The space program's primary "platform" is found not at the spaceport at Cape Canaveral, but in the armed war zone that is being constructed in Earth's outer orbit. While you, the human race, are being filled with dreams of new worlds and future migrations—of "giant steps for mankind"—they, descendants of the Annunaki, are attempting to tighten the shackles of your obedience and harness the suppressed energies of the human collective. These are the messages going out to the worlds that form your galactic 3D reality.

This, at a time when you are beginning to release from their hold, they still believe will be best accomplished by reconstructing the ancient electromagnetic grid that has bound you, as a subservient race, to their oppressive intention.

Ironically, the tighter they squeeze you, the freer you become.

The days of bloody ground battles and massive troop deployment are soon to pass into the oblivion of military history, to be replaced, amongst myriad "exotic weapons," by automatic triggers from space. Earth's outer orbit has already been encased in an absurd number of satellites, most of them spying devices patrolling all global frontiers ... and we observe that a new generation of "cutting edge" military technology has been launched into Gaia's weakening auric field within your calendar year of 2005.

The illusion of a future of peaceful co-existence on your planet is being constructed, it would appear, upon the architecture of a truly surrealistic military zone in space, from where ultra-high-resolution spy cameras, tracking mechanisms, and futuristic weapons systems are purportedly going to hold reign over the dark forces and the "enemies of peace." It is necessary, they are telling you, so that democracy—that illusive ideal—can reign supreme and so that "good" can triumph over "evil," keeping you all out of harm's way.

That, at least, is how the picture was recently painted for you, although since the irrational amplification of the fear zone has overtaken so much of your lives, the human race appears to be plunging headfirst into the icy waters of absolute military rule of the planet and of the space which surrounds you—while you continue to fund and prepare for the Space Wars scenario.

Where once fictitious space age spying devices and James Bond superheroes saved the free world from evil forces, it now seems electromagnetic field technology, satellite surveillance, and space-based lasers (sold to you as deterrents against the aggressor) are actually pointing down over your heads ... watching you, listening ... evaluating your behaviors.

Ironically, you, the "good guys," are under absolute scrutiny.

One of the most complex satellite spy networks is the Echelon system, so top-secret that it has evaded the scrutiny of many world leaders for decades, ever since its development during the cold war—that imposed state of military "balance" in your global political arenas. What should concern you is that the elaborate system is intended to target industries, businesses, organizations, and individuals, such as you, at every corner of the world—even there, in those countries you believe to be free nations, the pillars of the democratic ideal.

Echelon works, basically, by intercepting massive quantities of electronic communication (telephone, internet, fax messages) and then linking with top government computer networks in order to process them by means of an electronic "dictionary"— coded to pinpoint target words that can be considered threatening to the Power or disruptive to their plans. In essence, you are all vulnerable to this scrutiny, and so it is wise to bear in mind just how any controversial communications (those which are particularly unpopular with those who intend that you remain ignorant and powerless) will be considered by the individuals who are "listening."

Yes, indeed, Big Brother apparently feels the need to spy upon you.

Isn't it time you ask yourselves why?

As for the good and evil archetypes, look with discernment at those judgments, for the portraits of dark icons have all-too-often been painted for you with the blood of the innocent. As you become increasingly aware of the power structure's military manifestations, you realize that what you perceive as being perpetrated in the name of such lofty ideals as "freedom" and "peace" is, conversely, tyrannical and destructive—the cause of untold suffering across the globe.

The visible leaders of your world—the so-called "free" world—are leaping boldly towards a massive military penetration and occupation of Earth's orbital space and its immediate frontiers. We observe the secret construction sites on your planet and perceive their etheric projections in the no-time. They are making of Earth's environs a galactic battlefield where armed reconnaissance technology is aimed directly at you, just as it can be instantly directed outward—at the galactic community—upon command.

Should any **unwelcome** extraterrestrial craft enter the no-fly zone of your militarized globe, which blatantly refuses to participate in the great exchange of peaceful alien nations, it will simply be blasted out of earth space and destroyed.

Many already have been.

Many others have elected to simply stay away, avoiding contact with Earth, as they do other hostile environments in the galaxy.

It appears that mass consciousness upon your planet is still being distracted into believing that the Power's thrust into the unknown is truly about discovering new worlds and extending humanity's reach. Much is being made available to you from the scientific community regarding the possibility of life beyond your boundaries—but the truth is still predominantly lost to you. It has been categorized as a somewhat nebulous unreality, floating between science fiction and "remote" possibilities for future generations to explore ... but it seems that they still do not want you to believe that yours will be the generation to openly make clear and undeniable **contact.**

Of their true plans for space and earth controls, Dear Ones, absolute secrecy is held. Almost nothing is known of the reweaving of the ancient grid and the real purpose of the surveillance systems being actualized in space and within your recognizable boundaries.

You are not invited to even contemplate such secretive things.

By putting into place technology that can potentially control and alter your every thought, your every movement and every word, they believe they can bring the entire race to resonate with their lowest vibrations. They believe that Gaia herself can be entrained to the Nebiruan frequency, pulling that planet into orbit and through the vortex, and they are convinced they can keep that secret from you until their ends have been achieved . . . just as they presume that, like their Annunaki ancestors, they can keep the light of higher consciousness from penetrating their nets.

They are wrong.

Gaia's evolutionary energies and your own incredible brilliance are so exalted at this point in your ascension process that not even the darkest grid can suppress you or break your will in the final outcome.

Those who currently dictate earth affairs have made the strategic mistake of underestimating you, *Homo sapiens*.

They have tricked a segment of the population into believing that you are broken people . . . a dying civilization at the brink of annihilation. Apocalypse is their daily bread—everywhere violence appears to have replaced reason, compassion, and the ideals of your humanity.

However, they have forgotten how you manage, as a race, to

move swiftly beyond the stillness of adversity, just as they deny themselves the glory of universal love—love that permeates all dimensions: beyond time, beyond space, beyond darkness itself.

We wonder if you recognize that the plan to encase Earth's sacred outer being in intricate electromagnetic command systems has far more devious implications than the obvious military advantages it will provide the watchers who serve the power elite. What little they do tell you of improved strategic defenses is really a smokescreen and we suggest that you consider how and why Big Brother is so intent upon observing and listening to you as you react and mutate, as a population, to the frequencies they are raining down upon you, through your bodies, and into the cellular consciousness of every unit of your being.

This, because you still have not learned to say "no."

Globally, governments regularly intercept your personal conversations, copy your documents, and read your electronic mail— spying on whomever they wish ... whenever they wish. This, in the name of "national security," is justified to you as a means to maintaining stability in a world of terrorists, enemies, and "rogue states."

As for the new generation of surveillance satellites launched in 2005—pay attention. When these systems are in place, the global military intelligence community will be able to provide precise information not only of "enemy" movements around the globe, but of any **individual** on Planet Earth—any time, anywhere.

Is this not a blatant act of terrorism … or does the invasion of your sovereign rights not qualify as the darkest of intentions?

The United States, headquarters of the Secret Government, operates with relative freedom in space, masking its marauding about in the programs of its NASA operation, which your tax tithing funds entirely. The visible leaders are now aggressively preparing you to embrace and finance the construction of this disputed anti-ballistic system, which is supposed to serve solely as a deterrent against violators of peace on your planet—but which, instead, will be capable of overtly aggressive strikes against any and all select targets. Surely, you recognize that such power is no less ominous than your earlier discoveries of nuclear strike force, when the "peacekeeping" nation, America, dropped its atomic weapons in Japan.

Despite our observation of how your media control and manipulate your understanding of world events, it is still difficult for us to imagine that you, the people of Earth, have held such a limited memory of the staged Pearl Harbor incident and the nuclear retaliation that followed it as a "justified" response. We ask you to consider the potential of far more deadly weapons—Tesla particle beam death rays from space and scalar electronics—in those same hands.

Rest assured that what you are being asked to accept as a galactic defense system is absolutely **offensive** in every sense.

Let us move now into uncharted waters. We invite you to consider the potential that a space-based, armed communications network—one that is capable of beaming electromagnetic pulse technology to Earth—holds for mass mind control. Recall the

Woodpecker incident, to which we have referred in our earlier transmissions.* The question we wish to pose to you (and one we believe you must consider very carefully) is this: what if these highly sensitive devices can do more than merely "listen" and "observe" you? What if, instead, they can beam frequencies **at** you, as well as receive them **from** you?

Bear in mind that the masters of such technology are far more interested in manipulating you into acting in certain behaviors than they are in merely observing the behaviors themselves. If they can locate you, they can surely reach you—unless, by the nature of your intent and your focused will, you are simply scrambling their electromagnetic "messages." This is determined by the state of your mental/physical/emotional bodies, for if you are integral and operating in right mind—clear in your intent— such mechanisms can only marginally affect you ... if at all.

That, we assure you, is almost as easily done as it is said—if you are willing to sacrifice some of the "comforts" of modern technology and if you are capable of focusing your exquisite minds on the task at hand. It is our intention to provide you with the information that can help you disarm the perpetrators of darkness. This, while the Light Ones of higher realms work through us, adjusting your frequencies and lifting you into the light, is our purpose.

But only you can actually create the "safety" zone.

Only you can reach that place **within.**

⁚⁚⁛⁚⁚

---

* See *Atlantis Rising,* pp. 101–108.

As for control devices, know that it is not only from beyond Earth that you are being monitored. Consider how your use of bank credit cards defines your location as you move about, furthering your indebtedness to the Power—handing over your economic well-being, while providing a record of your movements, interests and purchasing power. Cellular telephones, proliferating everywhere on Earth, are satellite tracking devices of themselves. Your installation of electromagnetic devices for automatic billing on bridge and road tolls registers your movements. Surveillance cameras in places you wouldn't even imagine track and record your whereabouts and activities, while you go idly about your business, unaware that you are being scrutinized, observed, and investigated.

Electromagnetic locators in your animals, bar codes capable of transmitting information, sensors, satellites, cameras ... what in the world are you up to that is of such absolute interest to the appointed local and federal governments?

Big Brother is, indeed, watching you.

Let us show you some of what is in store for you in these next years.

You are being prepared for a cyberbionic reality that includes the implanting of computer chips directly into your neural networks—this is currently being played out as a "test" by government-owned scientists, but the technology has already been perfected in the intelligence agencies' laboratories and will soon be available to the public. This robotic technology involves the implanting of a sort of electromagnetically wired band that is designed to capture a bundle of nerve fibers. Once in place, it can be programmed to receive all manner of messages from the human nervous system and send them into a central computer program to be deciphered, coded and monitored—and **acted upon.**

You will clearly be capable of such banal exercises as executing computer commands merely by thinking them ... but who knows, say, how a surge of violent human emotion will transform into digital data? And if these impulses could be harnessed as electromagnetic frequencies ... what then?

Think, too, that the computerized micro-transmitting band will be capable not only of receiving neural impulses but also of imposing foreign electromagnetic frequencies, for the human neural network is just as much a receiver as it is a sender! You can understand how that could have you performing on command, like will-less robots. You might imagine how such technology could be utilized to evoke emotional responses that are not yours at all, as thoughts and commands could so be planted within you.

There are those of you who have come to believe that a number of political assassins are simply people who have been the subjects of such implants, and that they murder on command when the order is transmitted and received—and then translated in their disabled minds into a form of hypnotic obedience. We can confirm to you that this is, indeed, the case. The assassins of most of those peaceful leaders we have mentioned were such robotic killers—unwilling servants of the Secret Government. They are known to some of you by their code name: the Manchurian Candidates.

Consider what other possibilities arise from such technology

...and what other technologies emerge from those possibilities. It is a vicious circle—or rather, a downward spiral. There is no need for us to push your imagination—for the "edge" is forever moving to the foreground, and you need only observe what, until now, you have not wanted to see, nor dared imagine.

There is a pressing matter concerning the centralized classification system of the human race, which transcends all borders and national boundaries. All previous coding and numerical assignments, such as your tax tithing numbers, drivers' licenses, and identification codes, are soon to be replaced with a solitary barcode for every individual on the planet. It will be capable of registering every bit of data the Government considers relevant—so that your entire "bio" can be read electronically—and you are classified and warehoused, like global consumer products in your massive distribution networks.

The technology exists now, and unbeknownst to you, this form of human data processing and labeling—the barcoding of six billion individuals—has already entered its secondary phase. What you already know as the Universal Product Code, which now is found on all products of mass consumption, will soon be assigned to every individual—but with one significant difference.

The next generation of barcodes is actually of itself a sort of wireless communication system, capable of storing enormous amounts of information: **transmitting** data as well as receiving it. These will be used in the initial phase as data units, replacing traditional files and electronic databases, but the objective of the inventors is to eventually implant these barcode-tracking systems directly into your physical bodies—just as they have already begun to do with your animals.

These, Dear Ones, are but a few of the technologies that are surfacing, products of the power elite's intelligence agencies and military researchers. They are only a hint of what your "free world" leaders have in store for you.

What actions can be taken to diffuse them?

- Remember that no matter how powerful these aggressive technologies are, they cannot infiltrate your light shields— the setting of your intention that nothing enter you that is not of the Highest Order. Now more than ever it will be important that you work with these levels of soul protection and focused will. Call upon the Family of Light, and we shall rally the Higher Beings to help serve that purpose; recognize your spirit guides and the Angelic Beings, who hover about you; call every cell of your body to absolute integrity, clarity of purpose, and intent.

- Begin a daily regime of psychically clearing your mind, body, and soul—cleansing the auric field and declaring that all thoughts be yours and yours alone. The healthy aura serves as an inviolable barrier, but you must cleanse it of all the accumulated debris and repair the tears and holes that have come from ignoring, for so long, that you are multidimensional beings. Never forget that your etheric body **creates** the physical.

- Utilize the following invocation, when you first awaken to morning and when you prepare to enter the dream state (in which you leave your bodies, moving about on the astral):

"I call upon the Family of Light, asking to be surrounded in an impenetrable blanket of pure white light.

As a sovereign being, I intend that this brilliance hold as a barrier against any energies that are not of the Highest Order, and I invoke you, Angel Warriors of Light, to guide that process.

Let all other vibrations return to their point of emergence, carrying back to source the heightened energies of Universal Love."

- Resist, as best you can, the drug of electronics in your personal and business lives. Beware of enticing new electronic gadgets, asking yourselves if they are really necessary in your lives or if they are merely trappings that you can do without.
- Eliminate credit consumerism (it can be done!) and pay cash wherever you can, or better yet ... barter with others for goods and services.
- Wherever possible, boycott electronic devices—particularly those that involve satellite technology, such as surveillance security systems for your home and cars and satellite dishes for your televisions and radios. **The satellites must come down.**
- When you do communicate via electronic devices, use abbreviations and coded words for those highly sensitive subjects that could catch the eyes of the Echelon networks.
- Help raise the voice of protest against the campaign for human militarization of space by sharing your knowledge and pledging your commitment to peaceful rebellion.
- Support small merchants, cooperatives, and local markets. Without them, your communities will give way completely

to mass consumerism, and that only accelerates your global acceptance of the barcoding of human beings, while dehumanizing you in many other ways.

- Go to the trees. You are most protected when there are great boughs overhead, deep roots below you. If you are city dwellers, find the space for green plants on your terraces and in your homes; if you have found the way to live near nature, be sure to plant trees, giving back to the Earth what is being torn asunder.

- Believe in your sovereignty in every moment, and remember to speak it in every word, to own it with every breath, in every aspect of your lives. This is the way of the free-will being.

- Stay close to the earth. Find your way to the oceans and woods, for you must never forget that you are the Children of Gaia.

- Be aware of the elemental spirits: the sylphs, the glycines, the gnomes, and the salamanders. They are the nature of Earth as they are the human form—no less than the great Archangels, no less than the ascended masters, whom you worship. Remember that all is One in the Cosmos of Soul.

- Remember that your souls are **eternal**—sparks of light that have come, oh so briefly, to crystal in the physical matrix only to return to the Light, just as snowflakes evanesce in the stream.

10

Media and Mass Mind Control

We observe how the human race is subjected to constant and violent psychological bombardment from all manner of advertising and aggressive iconography—designer illusions that imprint products, ideas, and political opinion onto the mind screens of your souls. They are everywhere about you: on the streets, in the subways and buses, in the media, in your home and office environments.

The invasion of advertising and sociopolitical propaganda of those who wish to manage the human race is all-consuming, penetrating every aspect of your daily lives. Indeed, the controlling forces of your societies have imposed a form of consumption overload upon you, delivering millions upon millions of commercial messages via television, radio, the Internet, billboards, and printed press—and your stimulated sensory receptors pick up every single bit . . . every day . . . every waking hour of your lives.

So all-consuming is the media war being waged upon humanity that you are simply unable to escape it—as long as you remain active participants of your "civilized" world.

We are not suggesting that you behave as hermits, retreating from society to the caves of absolute isolation. Indeed, it is from the caverns that we wish to draw you into the full light of day.

But we do believe that you can actively diminish the effect such ferocious campaigning is having upon you—once you understand and consciously dissect the motives and methodology driving the advertising industry, which forms public opinion through false and distorted global perceptions.

You can then take back whatever you have been giving over to the media—as individuals, as "target" groups, and as a people—to eventually alter the impact the military/industrial complex is having upon the whole of the human race. You can abort their mission of mass mind control through your cultivated awareness, while contributing to a heightened public consciousness. In so doing, you will be retrieving fragments of your identity and reintegrating on many levels, contributing to the progress of society and the healing of Gaia.

Ours is a call for you to reclaim your sovereignty by liberating your minds—for once and forever—from all imposed control channels currently operating in your realm.

We are eager to be a part of that process—in whatever way we can—whenever you decide you are ready to open your eyes and rise up from your servitude, no longer blind and silent servants of the ruling elite.

Your search for liberation from the dark influence of the establishment begins with your willingness to consciously dedicate time and attention to the glaring problems facing your civilization. It involves expanding your perception from your personal realities to a more universal perspective and then bringing it back in again—that you may create and manifest right thought and action in your immediate world. It requires that you be willing and determined to scrutinize what is being either blasted or subtly filtered into your consciousness, for in so doing you learn how the external reality affects not only your inner peace but also the harmony of Gaia.

It means that you are going to have to look and listen to advertising in its overt and subliminal, Freudian forms like you never have before.

Hopefully, you will slowly extract yourselves from the inane programming and superficial icons of television, radio, and magazines, as well as the constant negative entrainment of your newspapers—all designed as backdrops for the selling of product and the targeted forming of public opinion. As you do, you will feel increasingly uplifted; you will feel liberated on many levels. You will realize your lives are fuller and more meaningful without the incessant intrusion of advertising, and a subtle calm will wash over your minds, no longer battered and torn by the emotional pull of its de-humanizing and manipulative messages.

You will have more time to nourish yourselves and to pursue more lofty thoughts—thoughts of what is truly important to your lives and how you can share your vision with the rest of the human race.

Personal freedom and the spiritual progression of any civilization are formed from a fundamental understanding of how every thought affects and creates the greater reality—just as the global reality imprints the personal experience. Remember: all aspects, dimensions, and realities are merely reflections of the One—the All That Is. So are you all; so are we.

So is the darkness; so is the light.

Never, not even for a moment, do you exist in a state of separateness: not at birth, when your spirit takes form by crystallizing soul consciousness as matter; not in death, when you shed your weighty sheath and take wing; not now, as you walk as physical beings in the world of *samsara*.

We know how you desire to shut out the frightening, unthinkable acts and consequences that are currently raining down terror upon your world. We understand why you prefer not to acknowledge or even contemplate the manifestation of evil, Dear Ones—but ignoring the dark side of reality is not going to make it go away. Like all suppressed energies, the fear only festers within you, like the most insipid malignancy—growing grotesque and mammoth as it lingers deep in those murky waters of your emotional reservoirs.

The truth is that your journey into the light eventually brings you to look at all the shades of shadow and experience the many layers of density, just as the Buddha explored and experienced human suffering before attaining enlightenment.

These aspects—the dark and malevolent doings taking place just outside of your experience—may not touch you personally, but they touch others, and so, by nature of the oneness of all things, they do qualify as **your experience.**

On levels you may have yet to understand, this is as much your karma as it is of those directly involved, which is why you made the cosmic appointment to take part in the great events unfolding on Planet Earth at this time. And so, we ask you to peer boldly into the dark corners, rather than fear the unknown and the "unthinkable"—for there is no better way to truly heal and move past the shadow.

We encourage you to overcome your blanket denial of what seem to be insurmountable evils, for you can and do effect change and alter reality in every moment of your lives. This you do most effectively when you are operating in the light of conscious awareness.

You must never lose sight of that.

You must never believe you are helpless in the hands of the Power.

⁂

A crucial aspect of this particular phase of your liberation involves developing a clearer understanding of how global advertising is designed to create wealth and power for the elite, while controlling you, the "masses," through mind-numbing and manipulative images and sounds.

You do realize and understand that the mainstream media exist merely to provide the corporate giants a vehicle from which they can drive their messages into your minds, creating local, national, and global markets for their goods. You see how the media exaggerate and perpetuate conflict and doomsday material to hold you paralyzed in fear, glued to your sets and newspapers, sitting-duck targets for their corporate sponsors.

This you do understand, don't you?

It is essential that you recognize one fundamental principle: because advertising finances media, it dictates what you see and hear through its various projections and venues—omniscient invaders of your sovereignty. It affects what you desire and how you express that need, what you buy and how much you consume, and how you think—insipidly robbing you of your ability to decide (of your own volition and free will) what is good for you. The greater whole is, in such a way, steered in the direction the Power wishes to drive society ... for the express interests of the elite who rule your world.

Such control mechanisms you might expect to find in a totalitarian state, but could you ever have imagined that you would be so programmed and de-humanized there ... where you still believe yourselves **represented** by your government, rather than manipulated by it?

More of you are becoming aware of the part advertising has played in the uncontrolled global explosion of mass consumerism, but you may not have a clear understanding of how corporate management teams use it to manipulate you at the subconscious level, selling you without your "conscious" consent or worse—creating desire and frustration at the unconscious level. Indeed, there is an overriding trend in contemporary advertising to attack and alter your libidos, activating the animal response and numbing the intellect.

How does advertising distort your reality? Let us explore this phenomenon as it regards the veritable war that is being waged upon the collective unconscious of the entire human race.

The fundamental requirement for the creation of a consumption population—a "throwaway" society—is the stirring of the populace into a state of escalating desire and diminishing self-worth ... a sense of "lack." You are marketed into believing that you are never "enough" so that you will believe you can never have enough. In this way, you will keep buying and believing what you are fed as the "solutions" to what is causing you to feel inadequate, inferior, and afraid.

This is what sells, pure and simple.

Manipulative advertising campaigns are designed not only for the corporations that produce consumer goods for global distribution. Your governments advertise and market you to embrace their philosophies and political abstractions by adhering to that very basic marketing fundamental: the creation of a sense of scarcity and the stimulation of your desire to fill the illusory void. Persuasive thought implants and subliminal messages are tools of the architects who design the puppet leaders' political speeches, build their campaigns, create the advertising, and sell you on nationalistic fervor and patriotic ideals.

Considering the information you have already acquired regarding the strategies of the New World Order, you can surely recognize how the Power manipulates the media in order to put its agenda of global domination into place on Planet Earth.

If you believe that your country is not safe from the "enemy," then you will buy the idea that a space-based anti-ballistic missile system will protect you—and you, the taxpayers, will finance it. If you can be convinced you are running out of energy, you will agree to unnecessary drilling for fuel in the last of Earth's sanctuaries: the diminishing habitats of endangered species, the protected forests, the marine environments.

The Power has accelerated the environmentally disastrous campaign of wanton (and unnecessary) drilling for fossil fuels, and you cannot but be concerned. It is being waged not only against the American citizenry but also against the entire global population—the planet itself—for in nature there are no arbitrary borders … just as there is no natural "separation." All is interdependent; all is connected.

The power elite knows all-too-well.

So do the animals, the plants, and the minerals.

It seems that only the human race, the "most intelligent" species of Earth, has forgotten what Gaia has always known and has attempted, in every way, to teach her children—the ones with the "superior" minds.

And so, despite the outcry of your most devoted ecologists and environmentalists, the Power's appeal to your collective fear of scarcity is so driving and so masterfully articulated that the petroleum lords dare to push you to the limits. If they are to have their way over you, a horizon of pristine forests and sapphire seas in Alaska's wildlife refuges will be obliterated by the grotesque blackness of the rapist's steel drills and towering oil infernos.

Now we ask you: is the politically motivated manipulation of your psyches any different than the commercial application of advertising for more specific financial interests, whereby you are sold, say, that you are not young-looking enough, so that you will buy their overpriced face creams, make-up, and other beauty products?

Advertising is the business of persuasion by illusion, whereby you are presented with images that appear to the conscious mind as harmlessly clever, provocative, or simply entertaining, but which conspire (at the subconscious level) against your free will. This insipid manipulation of your power centers can be far more harmful than you can imagine, particularly now—when you are determined to release yourselves from all controlling mechanisms and walk in the light of your absolute freedom of body, mind, and spirit.

It is designed to activate your desire, which is being perennially stimulated at the lower mental, physical, and emotional levels—so that you will buy the products that purport to resolve the states of disharmony that such constant bombardment of your psyches creates.

Advertising can also persuade you to adhere to a stereotype, a dogma, or a mindset. It can incite you to embrace political doctrines, justify war, and set the fashion dictates of global corporate interests. Indeed, through its practice of mind-controlling advertising, the industrial complex of the ruling class has waged an all-out assault upon you. They know how their overt messages and the subliminals planted within them alter your subconscious desire, affecting the economic, cultural, and even sexual standards of your societies.

As far as these messages are intended to reach you at a conscious level, where you are able to accept or reject them at will, it can be said that they are invasive and upsetting to the spirit, but we would not define them as *mind-control methodologies,* per se. We would not consider overt advertising (in its honest form) a "manipulation" of the mind and spirit, however influential it is upon human behavior—for you are responsible for what you consciously allow into your minds. You are the screening agents, and you alone decide what you deem worthy of consideration or relevant to your experience.

When, however, advertisers employ techniques that involve

the covert use of subliminal sounds and embedded images upon the subconscious, that is a quite a different matter.

Hidden to the conscious mind, such implants are a deliberate form of mind-control technology—technology that denies you that free-will faculty of selection and elimination of the endless "input" of images and data that daily attack and filter into your consciousness. Their widespread application in advertising and broadcasting denies your sovereignty as individual units of the All That Is and as vital members of earth society.

Isn't it time that you pay just a little more attention to how their overt and subliminal messages are altering your awareness—as individuals and societies?

We observe how your wealthy nations' current perception of fashion, which embodies every aspect of physical beauty, has determined that "chic" is necessarily reserved for the drastically underweight (not the starving, of course, for there is nothing elegant about famine and poverty by your social standards). Indeed, it is in those overfed, wealthier populations that "thin" has become the standard of beauty and elegance, as if the deliberately diminished form somehow signals a mastery of the physical being (whereas the starving poor are seen as victims of social injustice).

Ironically, in those wealthy societies, people are fatter than ever before.

The leaders of the fashion industry go to enormous lengths to entrain you to obsess on unrealistic icons of beauty, where pubescent youth represent the models of that unattainable perfection that keeps you buying skin- and hair-care products, pharmaceuticals, fitness equipment, chemicals, and industrialized "fat-free" foods. In a parallel reality, the commercial food industry is gorging you and your children on nutritionless, chemically enhanced fat foods and sugars.

As a mass, you have embraced the "fast food" industry, filling yourselves and your families with horrific chemical food stuffs and creating incredible "dis-ease" at the individual and societal levels.

Meanwhile, the icons of beauty in fashion advertising dictate the unrealistic standards to which society must aspire, but which only a minute percentage of the population can achieve. Does this not register as a paradox in your minds?

⁂

To assure that what you see portrayed in advertising is how you will believe you **must be,** subliminal graphic images are implanted into the artwork of the ads—messages that serve as powerful triggers for your unguarded subconscious minds.

Open any magazine and observe the advertisements. Relax your eyes and ask to be shown not what the mind believes it is seeing in the graphic but rather what is being activated in the subconscious by the hidden messages there.

Look beyond edges and outlines (as the human eye identifies form), into the shadows and the reflections in the imagery. Go deep—beyond face value. Ask yourselves: what am I being sold here? How am I being activated psychologically to believe I must have this product or that other? What is the underlying message?

Study the way the products are being presented to you and how the advertisement is emotionally manipulative and exploiting. When you look—truly look at what is being placed before you—you can **see** beyond the illusion. Identify the triggers that are being used there. As you train your mind's eye, the embedded images, designs, and letters will slowly become visible to you. These have been planted deliberately for your subconscious minds to perceive and internalize while the conscious mind is being teased into accepting what is on the surface.

Once you have trained yourselves to release the hold your conscious minds have upon what they believe they are seeing, you will find you cannot help but see such subliminal implants in most advertising. The most common range from the use of words (such as SEX) etched into the background to the use of suggestive masks and icons that are perceived at the subconscious level, regardless of your conscious awareness of them. They are there to activate your survival, sexual, and power centers, and they are designed to stimulate your animal desire, your irrational fear, and an unquenchable need that can never be satisfied!

They are there to ensure that you remain manageable consumers and willing slaves.

Subliminal sound messages are overlaid into the audio of television commercials, imperceptible to the conscious but perceived at the subconscious level. They are also transmitted via the Internet—you are just beginning to recognize the dark potential of such technology.

Imagine the power of being able to broadcast hypnotic suggestions or commands to millions of viewers without their slightest awareness? This technology has existed for some time now, and it has been tested not only upon individuals but also on pockets of the society, without your consent and without your knowledge that such insipid manipulations of the free-will zone are taking place right under your collective noses.

What if the subliminal message were to "obey," or to "go to war," or to "kill"? You are told, of course, that no such technology exists. No advertising agency will admit to using these covert and manipulative tactics, and yet you experienced them back when the dark forces circulated their test fear film, *The Exorcist*. That exercise involved creating study groups of audiences, who were the guinea pigs of some of the first widespread applications of subliminal sound overlays.

Your response to that level of sound and embedded graphic images was monitored, registered, and analyzed, setting the groundwork for much of the methods being used against you in today's advertising and media programming.

This, in our understanding of universal law, constitutes an invasion of the free will of sentient beings ... and it is anything **but** "democratic."

We believe it is time that you bring this assault of your lower energy centers up to full awareness, as part of the preliminary to your preparation for ascension. Once you see with your conscious minds that which is being planted in the subconscious, you will be free to reject it. In so doing, you strengthen your experience and understanding of **true freedom,** while emitting crystal clear waves of heightened vibrations from your enlightened minds ... waves of integral mind that are washing over the dams that for far too long have restrained the flow of human consciousness. This river of human spirit, free to run its true course, will cleanse the earth zone of the dark waters and their reflection in your collective soul.

When you, as conscious individuals, make manifest that which you perceive at the conceptual level, you serve as beacons for those who are still seeking the way. Empowered by your discoveries, you facilitate the process that releases you from the clutches of those who would enter your etheric bodies to manipulate and dictate your behavior. Thus, as individual units of the greater whole of humanity, you empower yourselves, raising the vibration of the collective unconscious.

We ask that you observe and analyze five minutes of television advertising. Make this a conscious experiment—a learning process. Consider a number of peripheral aspects, making note of the quantity of advertisements comprising the commercial "break" in the television programming. Record the duration of each and the number of back-to-back spots presented.

You will immediately realize that most of your television viewing is dominated by advertising rather than by the programs themselves.

Be aware of how the sound volume is raised at the onset of the advertisement sequence and how it then returns to "normal" when the regular program is back on air. This is one of the more easily recognized examples of subliminal manipulation: the television programmers are assuring their advertisers that you are going to listen to their message—or rather, that you are going to **hear** it.

We cannot stress enough the importance of being aware of what is around you and of seeing and hearing the underlying messages that are being imprinted upon your receptive minds. Now, at a time when the restrictions against such subliminal controls are being lifted and the governments are freed from the scrutiny of civil liberties vigilantes, you are going to have to create your own safeguards—and those of the children.

It is essential that you be freed of such invasive mind-control technologies if you are to achieve your mind's true liberation, bringing the Wisdom into focus and contributing to the communal good—the Light Alliance that is working its razor-sharp brilliance through the density and darkness.

Unfortunately, the mainstream is still so blindly infatuated with the earth-grounded electromagnetic grid that most have yet to recognize it for what it truly is ... but that, too, is about to change. As you have seen with the drastic devaluation of the technology markets—they have simply pushed you too far, over-estimating your appetite for virtual unreality and forgetting how you so love to play and gather in the great outdoors, dance in the sun, and bask in the moonlight, worshipping all that is right about your world.

We call upon you to use great discretion when approaching the Internet vehicle. It is of great importance that you take the time to prepare yourselves spiritually, mentally, and emotionally and to protect your energy fields whenever you enter this technology web. You can significantly alter the vibrational fields coming from your computers and entering others by willing that your thoughts' intention be to raise the intention of all conscious "travelers" moving along those wires.

This can be accomplished effortlessly, whenever you "log on" to the net, by first stating your intent and purpose ... in a manner such as this:

"As I enter here, I ask to be surrounded in the White Light, calling upon my Spirit Warriors to shield me from all vibrations that are not of the Highest Order, and asking that those unwelcome energies be bounced back to their source—as is appropriate to their evolutionary pace.

I send my grounding cord into the below, dropping like an anchor deep within the body of the Mother, as I hook solidly to the Earth.

And as I embark upon this journey, I ask that the Light Ones guide the way, infusing the grid with the light strings of the Universe."

We suggest that you:

- Dedicate some serious time to analyzing your media. Observe in full consciousness the overt messages that appear in advertisements and their actual relationship to the products being sold. Study and record your impressions. How do they make you feel? What is the underlying message? How are you being persuaded or manipulated, and on what levels of consciousness do you respond?

- Record your discoveries. It will serve your process of learning how to decode and disarm mind-control technologies and assist you in helping others broaden their awareness.

- Whenever possible, scrutinize ads for embedded words (SEX, WAR), mask-like images, animals, and demonic images and bring them to full consciousness. In no time, your trained eye will instantly extract the subliminals, and you will soon see clearly what is being broadcast into the collective unconscious.

- Write and petition the media as to your objection of manipulative and subliminal advertising—let them know you **know** and that you refuse to purchase their products because of it. Remember that you are six billion; they are two thousand.

- Write to the advertisers utilizing subliminals that you intend to boycott their products. Write to consumer interest groups and associations—and to the politicians.

- Write to the broadcasters that you intend to boycott their programming as a protest to the use of subliminal advertising by their sponsors.

- Write to the companies that produce the goods and services and voice your boycotting of their products until subliminals are removed from their advertising methodologies.

- Extract yourselves: limit your television viewing or cease altogether and be sure to monitor the children. They are the most susceptible targets, and they need your discernment as loving guardians of their developing minds.

- If you must watch television, boycott all advertisements by muting the voice and walking away while they are being aired.

- Trade in your gossip magazines and other meaningless, brainless reading materials for works of poetry, literature, and the noble mind.

- Do not allow your brilliant minds to atrophy by yielding to the brain-numbing abstractions that proliferate in your societies.

  Reduce your purchasing of consumer goods, recycling and repairing what need not be thrown away.

- Consider that wearing designer T-shirts and bags is free advertising for the industry. Do you wish for you and your children to serve as walking billboards?

- Be wise, be discerning, and be aware of what you allow to infiltrate your mental bodies. Knowledge is your liberation.
- Share your observations and insights with others, raising the flame, Dear Ones ... stoking the fire of human consciousness.
- Intend that your sovereign rights be upheld and that you always act of free will and conscious mind.

11

Air, Water, and Food:
Your Sustenance

The beginning of the new millennium marks a more critical phase of ecological imbalance on your planet, of which most conscious earth citizens are developing a forced sense of awareness. Despite the overwhelming denial of the "decision makers," whose abuse of Earth's resources knows no limits, the signs surround you, as Gaia storms her rebellious rage upon the winds, waters, and desert sands.

What you have termed the "food chain"—that exquisite balance in nature, which feeds life and consumes decay (from the minutia of viral and bacterial forms to you, the ultimate consumers in the food pyramid)—has been inexorably altered by the poisoning of entire ecosystems at every point of your vast planet. The toxicity of your unprocessed waste has smeared the sky, the sea, and the earth with blackness—the color of human ignorance.

For millennia, Gaia has rebounded, cleansing and healing what humankind has created … but never before has your abuse been so total and unrelenting. Warriors of the New Frontier, you are now in the thick of it, experiencing the initiation of Earth's imminent resolution.

Yet, although the human race has finally begun to recognize the results of its defilement of the Earth, only a very small percentage of human beings actually takes any constructive measures to improve the global condition.

Examine your individual behaviors. Can you truthfully declare that you are actively working for the environment—contributing to the healing of Gaia? You, the lightworkers of your realm, devote much-needed energy to meditation and prayer, and that is essential—but on more "earthly" terms ... have you been willing to sacrifice your comfort zones and limit your wasteful activities? Gaze honestly into the mirror. Have you reduced your consumption of fuel, conserved water, or planted a tree? Have you unplugged your microwave ovens, silenced your televisions, and lowered the volume of your noise?

Remember that Earth is a living organism, enveloped and permeated by definitive vibrational fields of electromagnetism, gravity, and other subtle energies, which define the properties of consciousness and matter as they interact and co-create in your realm. Like you, the celestial deities (co-creators of the Universe) are subject to certain laws of physics, as they are particular to your solar system, to the physical universe, and to the Cosmos in its entirety. The energy fields that rule Earth directly affect these aspects in you; they interact with the life energies of all living things on your planet.

We ride the waves of your thoughts—particularly those of the awake and alert there on your planet—and we ascertain that you understand how the polluting of the air, water, and earth alters these energies, thereby diminishing the life force of Gaia and her ability to maintain the balance. We see that you understand the circle of events that such abuse creates, as the karmic wheel of Earth's material existence spins through "time." You realize that the more Gaia chokes in the muck, the more you, too, struggle to breathe. The pranic flow is suppressed. The rainbow of life fades, blanketed in the dense greyness of new storms that are rising.

You realize that the leaders are only pretending when they unite in the great halls and that they simply are not going to rally for Gaia. They blatantly refuse to do it, and that is their mandate as much as it is their personal interest, for almost all of them have sold their souls to reach those levels of wealth and personal power. Let it not be forgotten that they are operatives of the Annunaki, whose only interest in Planet Earth is its key to the survival of their home planet Nebiru, as we have described it to you in the text of *Atlantis Rising*.

It is clearly the people who will have to take action, and you, the lightworkers, have been called to lead the way. As the Awakeners, you have heard the trumpets sound, and that is as you decreed it—many lifetimes, many moons, many star systems ago.

Soon, very soon now, your solar system will enter the more dramatic phases of ascension, and it will be of the utmost importance that you heal the clamorous disharmony that sounds from Gaia's gut. For the sake of that new reality, you will want to deliver unto the higher realms **not** a charred and dying planet— the reflection of humanity's abuse—but rather a life-nurturing deity who radiates the love and the light of so many growing numbers of awakening starseed.

If that is your intention, then time it is that you stand for one principle—a conscious commitment to the betterment of your world and the nesting of conscious seeds that will manifest in new life as Gaia surges forward, seeking higher ground.

Stand tall and firm, like the great oak trees, rooted to the soul of Gaia—your arms reaching toward the stars. Let there be a greater sense of what will come forward from you, and from all the children of Planet Earth, from every living being of your world—even the shadow seekers … as Gaia emerges.

As you develop the multidimensional perspective, you realize that you can and do lightwork from many levels, and this is exciting to you, as much as it is bewildering—due to the limitations of your 3D experience. On a practical level, you can perform specific actions that are clearly beneficial to the environment; you are aware of the ecological considerations that each individual can contribute as part and process of Earth's transmutation. These ideas and capabilities—your illuminations and inspiration—you can bring to the local community, and the community, however small, can affect the greater whole and so on, throughout the Universe.

On higher levels of consciousness, where you operate from other lifetimes or from a "future" existence, you imprint your earthly experience with thought emanating from those simultaneous realities in which you co-exist and operate, imprinting or crystallizing in your material reality. As former Atlanteans, for example, many of you overlay the terror of the ultimate experience upon your current understanding of earth evolution, which is one overriding reason why there is so much fear to be resolved at this juncture. Yet other Atlanteans, those of the Golden Era, are imprinting their conscious awareness of the crystal beings with the wisdom of the ancient ones, opening portals in the collective unconscious.

As multidimensional beings, you already exist in many dimensions and hold consciousness at many points on the time-space continuum, and this omnipresence you do express in your current walk-through in myriad ways—expressions of how you deal with your world and your own feelings of permanence ... of survival.

Other ways that you imprint the reality of your now and your perception of the human condition are born from your experience of that place in the no-time (that you would consider a "future" reality), where you have already experienced the ascension of your solar system. From that vantage point, you realize that there exists only a subtle veil separating that part of you that has already passed from the time barrier of 3D from the you that is moving about in this reality—the illusory framework of the universe of matter.

With the mutation of your DNA, which is beginning to occur for many earth beings, this is becoming much clearer to you, enabling you to achieve far greater focus and clarity of intention ... and that is one truly remarkable reflection of the wonder of who you are and the splendor that awaits you.

Air

In the hierarchy of needs that defines human survival on Earth (in its physical manifestation), oxygen is the most significant requirement for life. You may exist for weeks without food, days without water, but only a few minutes without air, whose elemental deities provide the spiritual transportation vehicle, in a sense, of *prana*—the life force of all consciousness.

Those who understand the significance of proper breathing and the respiration of prana clearly recognize how air and breath constitute the essence of your physical existence. That it is possible to exist solely through rhythmic breathing and expiration of prana is one of the secrets that has for so long eluded you, but which is now coming to consciousness as you prepare for light-body awakening. Only the most devoted initiates have currently reached this state of physical "enlightenment" (surviving in physical reality solely through mastery of breathing)—but as more of you consciously prepare the body for ascension, the significance of correct breathing will become absolutely clear to you.

This cannot be sustained in locations where the air is highly toxic, as it is in densely populated urban areas. The air quality of most of your cities and urban zones is far worse than you are being led to believe, although even the highest mountain peaks are glazed in the drizzle of such poisons.

It is not an overstatement to tell you that if you are living in or near cities and industrial zones, you are suffering from carbon monoxide poisoning and the inhalation of other chemicals in alarming quantities. The lack of oxygen and diminishing life force in the air you breathe is affecting your personalities, your health, and your social behavior.

It is altering your make-up at the cellular level, for every unit of your being requires and is nourished by the breath of life, which is drawn into your being and released in cosmometrical forms and vibrational patterns of universal design.

The unprecedented acceleration of respiratory illness, allergic conditions, and lung disease is directly related to the breakdown of these sacred patterns, which is being exacerbated by the exploitation of the environment: the cocktail of gases permeating the atmosphere; the pollution of the oceans, lakes and rivers; excessive emissions of carbon monoxide and toxic elements in cities and industrial areas; the spraying of chemicals over vast areas of your skies; the HAARP Project; the burning of tree populations and the diminishing flora—the lungs of Gaia.

And so, if you must live in urban centers, it is of utmost importance that you establish a way to improve your air quality. If, instead, you have made the lifestyle choices which will allow you to immerse yourself in nature, do remember to respect and nurture the environment with every thought, every act, and every step.

Your life breath, the primary essence of your survival, depends upon it.

Water

You are only now beginning to realize that Earth's once-abundant water supply is not infinite and that all of you are soon going to be faced with extreme water shortages and drought. There are those lands, places that are so remote to you that you are able to brush away the thought of them, where people, animals, and plants are already dying of thirst. Wars are being fought over water, and this problem will touch you personally far sooner than you can imagine.

While you, of the wealthy nations, mindlessly plunder and waste the elixir of life, people are dying of thirst and famine from the lack of crops, which can neither take seed nor come to harvest without the natural cyclical return of water.

Within a very brief time, the taps of more than one-fifth of the landmasses of Earth will run dry. We ask that you think of that, when you fastidiously wash your cars, luxuriate in the shower, fill your pools, flush your toilets, and leave the precious water flowing from the faucet in your distraction—believing, like good consumers, that there is no end to the "supply."

Regarding the quality of your drinking water, an entire manuscript could be written, and indeed, much qualified information is available to you. For our purposes here, we wish to draw your attention to the most pressing aspects of your consumption, always focused, as we are, on the energetic properties of all that with which you interact as physical and spiritual beings.

Almost seventy-five percent of your physical body is comprised of water, just like Planet Earth, of which each human being is but a microcosmic image. Water serves as the resonance field through which your cells communicate with each other, transferring data from the DNA and transmitting all matter of information via the waves. It is the conductor for the electrical activity of the cells; it is the highway of the cells' electromagnetic currents.

Water and its elemental spirits, the glycines, move through cell tissue, regenerating, nourishing the cellular units, and cleansing the waste and toxic elements that have accumulated within you. This is a physical phenomenon just as it is a spiritual process. As in the air you breathe, so water (in its life-enhancing, natural state) bears a cosmometric identity or pattern, which reflects the inherent consciousness of that element and resonates with the molecular nature of earth biology. This brilliant design, the sacred geometry of water and the manifestation of the consciousness that permeates the element, is disrupted in most of your commercial drinking water, which is tainted by metals, disinfectants, and other pathogens.

Knowing what you do about resonance and the conductive nature of the water in the human body, it should be clear to you that drinking water laden with metal residues, toxic chemicals (such as fluorides and chlorine), and bacteria is not health-enhancing in human beings—nor any other "natural" living organism, for that matter. Just as you are concerned about the effect the pollution of the oceans, rivers, and lakes is having upon the balance of Earth, so must you be concerned about what effect the water you regularly drink is having upon your well-being and how the water you pollute is affecting the health of Gaia.

Food

Here we wish to address the question of the food supply, which (through genetic and chemical manipulation of crops and animals) is becoming increasingly poisonous and deadly to human and animal organisms ... far more deadly than ever before.

We believe that those who choose to ignore or minimize the undeniable truth regarding the devastation of the global food supply are either misinformed or unconcerned for their personal health, and that is their free-will choice to make.

However, as conscious units of a greater being, each of you plays a part in the healing or destruction of the deity—just as the individual cells of your healthy body unite to fight off invasive viral and bacterial agents that would destroy the "sky," "sea," and "earth" of your human forms.

Therefore, we do call upon you, units of earth consciousness, to consider the overall health of Gaia and the effect widespread chemical spraying of crops, chemtrails, dumping of toxic waste and raw sewage, and the genetic manipulation of the food supply are having on all the living beings of your world. Then, as concerned citizens of many nations (whose governments, unfortunately, all serve the greater interests of global industry), you may give more consideration to the issues that we present here, becoming more aware of what is taking place and more consciously involved in what you feed your mental, emotional, and physical bodies. You may rebel, taking back the power over your own lives, beginning with what you bring into the physical body as "nourishment" of the soul.

In *The Cosmos of Soul,* we have suggested a simple structure to follow regarding your foods, bearing in mind that you will need to draw as much light into the body (at the cellular level) as possible, as you prepare for the process of evolving into light body. Insofar as the ingestion of food is concerned, this has been, until recently, best achieved by eating a high volume of fresh fruits and vegetables and the elimination of meat from the diet.

However, given what is being brewed in the laboratories of top-level industry, you must now examine with caution the quality and the origins of the plant foods and their end products now gracing the shelves of your favorite supermarkets.

You need to know that the meat supply is increasingly diseased and infectious. Despite the lies you are being fed by the media, meat producers are losing control over the spread of "mad cow syndrome," which has moved out of the restricted areas and crossed international borders—spreading from species to species, from cows to sheep and pigs. What is not infected carries growth hormones, enormous quantities of antibiotics, and adrenal overloads, and has been fed with genetically modified feed, also treated with toxic pesticides.

It is fear manifest, for every cell of the dying animal is filled with the terror of the slaughter, and you ingest this emotion. All of these unharmonious aspects are absorbed by your bodies (temples of the soul) every time you cut into the juicy steak or bite into the greasy, flavor-enhanced hamburger.

We are pleased to see that many more of you are now aware of these aspects of meat consumption and are moving away from it altogether.

North America leads the world in the cultivation and wide-scale distribution of genetically modified foods, much of which you are unaware that you are ingesting—for the industry clearly does not wish to stimulate your curiosity or product-resistance. Transgenetic seeds and crops are being imposed upon global markets, crossing over to healthy crops and threatening future food supplies, and yet these industries (and their lobbies) still manage to avoid having to provide detailed labeling and warnings for you—the consumers.

Those of you who have switched from dairy and meat to soy-based alternatives should know that over sixty percent of commercially available soy products have been genetically modified or chemically treated, so you are wise to buy only those which are clearly labeled and verified as **"organically grown."**

Corn, canola, dairy and potatoes—and their commercial end products—are the most likely foods to have been genetically modified. Awareness of this problem is slowly appearing in the media, but so much is hidden from you. You will have to give more of your individual attention to the question of the source and content of your foods, becoming far more discerning in your approach to food preparation and consumption.

Irradiated foods are proliferating in the supermarkets—particularly in the produce sectors. Trust that you do not want to bring radiation into the digestive track and that such foods do not enhance human health. Have you considered cultivating an organic garden? There, you will bring to your being the true nature of the food, its circadian rhythms, the live elements, and the light that is born within it.

The meat supply is dying—plain and simple. It is no longer the will of the animals to feed your insatiable hunger and submit any further to human abuse, which is why they have collectively committed to serving your awakening by leaving the planet in droves.

You hear daily warnings about the tremendous diseases appearing in cows, sheep, pigs, and let us not forget the diseases carried in poultry, ranging from various cancers to the deadly influenza virus that was first identified in the poultry markets of the Orient. Aside from the metaphysical question of the taking of meat into your bodies or the environmental aspects of such global consumption of animal flesh, there is an ever-increasing risk associated with the ingestion of meat. See if you can let it go and release from the darkness of dead animal flesh for once and forever.

Genetically modified foods can cause damage to the organs and most significantly they **destroy the immune system.**

We remind you that governments do not have your best interest at heart. Politicians serve their "generous" industrial lobbyists by enacting legislation that protects those corporate entities that would poison you in the name of **profit.** Therefore, do not be complacent, awaiting the approval from your central governments and their so-called consumer protection agencies, such as the Food and Drug Administration and its international equivalents. Do not be lulled into a false sense of security, believing that you are being cared for and looked after by the very ones who are poisoning you.

Children are particularly vulnerable, due to their consumption of dairy and the often excessive consumption of processed foods—many of which are corn or potato based. Processed cereals should be reduced substantially, if not eliminated, and chips and other snack foods are the worst offenders. Do you care enough about the health of your loved ones to remove these poisons from their clutches?

You see the drastic increase in allergic children and adults. Know that genetic manipulation dramatically increases the risk that the plant will develop toxic or allergy-causing elements.

One objective of genetic manipulation is to cause the plant to emit its own very high levels of pesticide, with the idea of creating an improved form of pest control in agriculture. Know that the levels of toxins being emitted are by far greater those that occur with spraying, and that these are far more damaging to the being. They can cause birth defects and lead to numerous malfunctions within the physical body.

Another objective of the industrial complex is to create genetically altered **drug-producing** foods. These you will hear referred to as "functional foods." While they are absolutely counterproductive to the health of the human organism, they are of great potential to the pharmaceutical industry's profit margins.

Genetic manipulation of animals, crops, and insect populations is devastating to the environment as well as human health. The flora of Earth know no boundaries, and the genetically altered crops are crossing over into the others, destroying the natural sequence of earth biology.

What can be done?

- Growing resistance to de-humanizing, global industrialization has begun to demonstrate itself in various parts of the world. Become involved. If your personal circumstances or beliefs do not allow you to be an activist, we do encourage you to be **aware** of the issues for which your brothers and sisters stand against the Power. These warriors are fighting for humankind, and although there will always be those who use the stage for their personal agendas, most are there to represent the human race. Whatever form you decide it will take, your support will raise the voice of consciousness.

- Wherever possible, grow your own produce. Those who are city-bound can join together in communal gardening projects; these are "sprouting up" in various places across the globe. Contact your local and regional offices for information. Investigate and support alternative food suppliers, such as health food stores and food cooperatives.

- Contact your supermarkets and express your concerns, letting them know that you are being forced to find alternatives to their stores in search of foods that are not genetically modified or irradiated.

- Write to your government representatives: the louder your voice, the greater the response—for they need you. They need public approval if they are to hold the seats of authority, no matter how secure they appear to be without it.

- Educate the children, bearing in mind that they are a highly valuable target group for the advertisers of junk foods. This means, however, that you must create the alternatives by dedicating more time to the selection, harvesting, and preparation of truly good-tasting, healthy food.
- Dispose of your microwave devices. They produce enormous amounts of electromagnetic radiation and, by their nature, encourage the consumption of pre-fabricated, plastic food— food that has little or no nutritional value.
- Boycott investing in companies that produce genetically modified crops and those that are developing biogenetic technology.

There is only so much that you can do if you remain insular and self-serving. Global solutions require global efforts, whereby you unite as an international force—the voice of the people.

You have begun to talk back to the Authority, and we commend you.

You have begun to raise the volume, and we hear you.

You have, indeed, begun to reclaim the power—and we are with you every step of the way.

> *Children, we call upon you*
> *to stand for yourselves and for each other*
> *for the plants and animals and all the living beings*
> *for Gaia.*
> *You are precious—lightworkers of Earth*
> *If not you, who then?*
> *Who will change your world?*

Part II
And the Veil Lifts

12

Shine the Wisdom...
Let the Light

The Overlighted Ones have joined with us...
we shall be raising the vibration.

Excellent teachers and spirit masters who have walked upon the Earth in various phases of human development and who appear throughout your written and mythical history have alluded to the "Secret Wisdom" but never openly shared it, for theirs were circumstances far different than those that are unfolding, now that the Earth Mother is moving into position and such expansion is occurring in the collective unconscious of the human race.

Theirs were times when secrecy was essential to their own protection and to safekeeping the knowledge of the true nature of man and the multidimensional Universe. It was necessary that they protect themselves from the retribution of the dark-intended—those disguised as academicians, priests, and kings. Theirs were times of initiation, challenge, and obstruction as much as they were illuminated, joyous, and guided by Angelic Beings, Light Ones, and intelligence from the highest realms and the heart of All That Is.

Indeed, theirs were times when your Solar Logos was firmly committed to the universe of matter, as was Earth and the family of deities who have shone in the brilliance of your Sun since its materialization in physical space … as was the mass of humankind.

Consider what we have told you of Atlantis, of its fall from glory in the hands of the Dark Priesthood, and it will be clear to you why so many manifestations of the spiritual and alchemical progress achieved during the apex points of your highest civilizations have been secreted and stored away—awaiting a time in your evolution when human consciousness would be capable of taking those giant steps and then leaping forward to claim its true heritage … to walk in the brilliance of enlightened mind and spirit.

That evolutionary point on the time-space continuum is **now.**

Your Solar System, the body of Ra, is transmuting at every level … there simply can no longer be any question about it. The Sun's radiations have increased dramatically. Some planets' light bodies are becoming more explosive; others are more luminous. The Universe is literally buzzing with the heightened frequencies of the celestial soul reaching higher.

The awakening can feel this great shift taking place; intellectuals can conceptualize it; your scientists are discovering ways to measure it. Indeed, all of the living beings of your world hold awareness, at some level, that this is like no other moment in Gaian history, and those of you who have explored your residual fear and worked through it are scintillating in new vibrations and the radiations that are actively regulating the shifting consciousness of the galaxy.

Your thoughts of wondrous new realities—of your transformation into light body—are every bit a part of this heightening awareness and its anchoring of the light as is Earth's painful (yet exhilarating) process of cleansing, renewal, and the preparatory geophysical changes that are reaching new extremes, as the planet spins rapidly towards the ascension "tunnel" at the vortex center.

Conversely, those who are manipulated by the dark force and who choose to cling to their misguided fears and other limiting emotions are frozen, in a sense, in their slowed vibrations—and here we wish to emphasize once again the importance of your commitment to recognizing how and why these energies are deliberately imposed upon the global society... and how they eventually take form in what you refer to as "core beliefs" of the collective.

While you are experiencing a quickening of your thought processes—your manifestation of thought to matter and your heightened emotional responses—those who are still bound to the illusions of physical reality and who cling to its impermanence (in fear and ignorance of what lies beyond) are going through an opposite, polar experience—one which freezes thought forms as templates upon which other negative vibrations can be implanted and find resonance ... one that shuts down the heart center and fortifies the ego self.

Drugs, as we have previously stated, are proliferating fast and furiously—"mood-controlling" remedies being thrust upon your societies as panaceas to the personal and cultural disharmony that is manifesting as a reaction to all that is being force-fed to you by the Power. Their effect, the numbing and intoxication of the mental and emotional bodies, is registered upon these templates, further slowing the mind's vibrational frequencies, until what resonates within the individual are barren thought forms that resemble the lake in winter, where frozen ice fields blanket the deep waters below.

These waters, mirrors of human emotion, remain trapped in a matrix of impure and inharmonious commonality, where glimpses of winter's oblique rays of light can be perceived upon the surface, but which are refracted by the density of that icy shield: never penetrating into the below and therefore never reaching resolution.

Those of you who have learned to live Center always walk with the light directly overhead. What is running through the crown and descending the spinal cord is **the Astral Tube,** bathing the chakric centers, filling the heart, and anchoring you to Earth in the nurturing warmth of the deity.

You know your help is needed to bring others into that direct light—where the conscious mind observes, confronts, and resolves the shadow and where the salve of illusion is supplanted by knowledge and the integrity of the soul.

Your fearless voice is the flute that will lead the lost and misguided out of the maze—no matter how convincingly they seem determined to remain there, confused and misguided at every turn of the labyrinth.

⁙

We wish to acknowledge, for once and forever, that your individual ascension process, the spiritual journey, is as much determined by your soul's unique progression as it is a reflection of your contribution and interaction with the community of the living. Your commitment to the greater whole and the work you are undertaking in your pursuit of spiritual advancement are propelled to great heights once you fully understand how your thoughts, the prime movers of your personal realities, reverberate throughout the Cosmos ... just as they crystallize, in the density of 3D, as matter.

If you believe you cannot effect change at the global level or that you do not wish to waste your time in any way serving others when you are so intent upon your own leaps and bounds along the upward spiral, then you are surely deluding yourselves when you contemplate the wonders of Spirit and your own potential.

Similarly, if you are unwilling to dissect and examine the mechanisms that bring shadow to human consciousness, then you will find it difficult to pass the tests of the great initiation, to walk the tightrope in perfect balance—fearless light bearers of the ascension.

We call upon you to be self-aware, forever observing how the ego preens in the limelight, and to be humble, never—not even for a moment—mistaking the glitter of your gifts and abilities for the brilliance that radiates from the heart.

This said, let us begin by recalling the once-secret Hermetic axiom:

> As above, so below
> and
> as below, so above

Upon this quintessential precept of universal law, we wish to build a clearer understanding of the nature of all consciousness and how this is reflected from that which exists beyond the subatomic particles, the cells, your beings, the Earth, your universe, the higher realms, and infinitely outward—traversing the sea of all existence—the All That Is.

Your global religions and limited scientific prowess have so dogmatized the nature and existence of Creation that most of you have embraced substantially rigid core beliefs as to the "beginnings" of the Universe, the planets, and your own biological birth into physical reality. Your understanding of the passing from that reality, the death process, is even more limiting—since you fear it so.

Hence, we believe that a most essential requirement to your understanding of the ascension process of man and deity, of passage from the illusory realm of 3D, is to bring you to some very clear observations of the entering and exiting from any given lifetime … because your believing in finite realities undermines your ability to perceive your own infinity and that which we have referred to as the "no-time" of all existence.

Consider your own birth—that emergence which you consider the "beginning" of your current lifetime. Let us mark the points of your passage. You chronicle your birth as the separation from the mother, and the date of this traumatic departure, which you burn into your mind's time record, the calendar, becomes your identity.

Astrologers and other readers of frequencies and celestial vibrations celebrate this time marker—it identifies your entry into the world and provides a schematic of stellar and planetary influences, which embody certain characteristics and distinct forces that will be at work during your walk through the physical lifetime.

But this is only a partial truth. What of the gestational months within the womb, when your physical form, the grouping of intelligent cellular units, reaches maturation? Simply because you cannot precisely identify the moment of fertilization, the union of the ovum and sperm, it seems your concept of birth and initiation into the physical life denies nine full lunar cycles in which you most definitely "exist." It is during that period that some of the most exquisite cosmometry, the great work of Creation, elaborates the design of your biological being.

Vedic astrologers do attempt to account for this transitional state of **being/becoming,** yet they are in a quandary as to the marking of the actual moment of "birth."

Let us investigate further. What of the "before" of that union ... the consciousness of the father's sperm, which knows no other objective than to spark the flame of new form by penetrating the yet unfertilized egg? Is there not intelligence and self-awareness in each? Does not the sperm, fully aware of its purpose, race forward—a creator in its own right, as does the egg await the connection and then, impregnated, intelligently and with unfaltering perfection, initiate the process of cellular reproduction? Surely there can be no finer example of absolute and totally focused intent!

Extend your awareness even further backwards (as we intend the "before" time frame), to that which exists prior to the sperm and egg ... and your mind naturally envisions your fully aware father and mother, conscious beings, carriers of the sperm and egg that united to trigger your entrance, and so did they too come to be, seed of their parents' seed—in the infinite cycle of regeneration.

You understand that your own birth is exquisitely infinite—

as is your death, when your body (the crystallization of spirit) dissolves its material form and the soul continues its journey along the spiral in that other direction, which you perceive as the "after" time sequence—but which is every much the "before" as is your **now.**

As you examine the processes of all life, you are shown over and over again that **there is no definitive beginning.** You simply cannot identify the initial spark in physical terms, for there is always a before and that which follows it: a form and then that form to thought, a thought and then that thought to the wave, the wave and then that wave as crystalline patterns to form again. And from that observation, the mind can only take the obvious leap—that neither is there an ending. And that is one aspect of the Hermetic axiom of which we speak.

Inherent in your perception of God, to whom we refer and with whom we resonate as "Prime Creator," there must (by nature of your limitation in the time paradigm) be a realization that the ultimate conscious Being, the initiator of all existence, has "thought" the Cosmos into being, but that "His" existence is the eternity—timeless, beginningless, and unending. Your understanding of such totality surely must embrace the idea that there simply is no point of departure, but rather an omnipresent, eternal order to all existence—the consciousness of the Universe and the Cosmic Soul.

Forget the big bang theory. That is scientific guesswork (something science is sworn never to do!), a spiritless vision—and a wrong conclusion.

Like the sperm, whose existence is but a continuum of every generation that came before and that will come after, consciousness is infinite—a reflection of the Paramount Intelligence, the Godhead, which never "began" and never will "end." And oh! This requires some serious thinking and a probing examination of your belief systems—for if you are to contemplate and absorb the meaning of such revelations, then you are going to have to rethink the true meaning not only of your personal lives, but of the entire Cosmos—of "God" itself.

Then, enlightened in the knowing that all is eternal and that the difficulties of your present situation are merely the labor pains of the Mother as you are all about to be birthed into yet another reality, you will look upon those difficult issues that we have brought to you with the knowing that they can and will be resolved, or transmuted, or absorbed into the All That Is, That Ever Was, and That Always Will Be. And you will go on to your next lessons, at whichever "place" in the Universe your soul will choose as its next training ground, and there, too, you will work for the highest good—always seeking that goodness that is within you and somewhere, however close or remote, within all others.

You want this now. You want to reach new levels of understanding, focused upon beauty and living love. And you know that, finally, the time of secrets, of coded messages and shrouded truths, has passed.

Gabriel has sounded his horn.

Now, as the veil is lifting, there are tears in your physical reality, and untold numbers of human beings are beginning to see the "other side"; you are communicating multidimensionally and bearing witness to your own magnificent soul extensions.

As you mature into this expansive awareness, you are moving beyond your fascination with phenomenon and delving far more deeply into the purpose of it all. The time of simply having fun with your gifts is past—that is a wrong use of your abilities, and they will eventually deceive you if you allow ego to deter you. As trumpeters of the New Dawn, you require these earned abilities in your service to the All, and it is for that purpose that, together with other servants of the light, we have come through for you—as you are coming through for us.

And that, too, is a reflection of Hermes's coded message: "As above, so below ... and as below, so above ..."

Let us remind you that a sliver of the physical universe, observed through a cosmic microscope, would demonstrate the same properties as microbiology in all its forms on Earth. Just like the cellular activity represented in your laboratories, that "sample" would react and mutate from the mere fact that it was interacting with the observer ... exchanging energies. The waves of consciousness that are created wherever one observes a given reality always alter the reality, affecting its evolution.

We, who exist beyond the physical realms, do observe the stars and celestial beings of the universe of matter in very much the same way as your scientists observe the microcosmic elements of biological life—for, from our perspective, the material realm in its entirety is the minutia.

From a perspective that is beyond anything but your wildest imaginings, the microscopic representation of a planet (were you to fathom such an immense viewpoint) is to the universe of matter just what a cell is to your body ... and it is "affected" by the extradimensional observer as are the cells in your lens altered by the earthly biologist. These dynamics have now been proven by the quantum scientists and biological technologists, whose experiments consistently demonstrate how the mere act of observing alters the outcome of the experiment: it alters the consciousness of the matter under the glass. This, in essence, is how consciousness alters matter and is the objective of many a dedicated alchemist.

This, too, is the above and below connection alluded to in the Secret Wisdom, and it is so simple and yet so remote to your understanding, merely because of your limited perspective.

And here we are, speaking to you through the channels that are required to help create the manifestation of our thoughts in decipherable messages that come to you in these—the glyphs of your modern communication codes. Your reading them affects the outcome of our message. How you perceive them affects the outcome. Your consciousness reacts to the information, rejects or embraces it, condemns or celebrates it to others, and becomes inexorably connected to it.

This ... all of this ... affects the outcome of our message and its manifestation in your world.

Here is an exquisite example of how the below serves the above. Do you recognize it? Your activated response, the personal experience, is reflected back into the community, and so how you perceive us and what you do with the information is just as important (if not more so) than the message itself.

Do you see this clearly? It is important that you understand how the dance unfolds, just as it is essential that you comprehend how these same processes define your interaction with all the living beings of your realm, when you contemplate your role in the evolving world in which you reside. It all ripples back—across the cosmic sea—affecting every aspect of the multidimensional Universe.

Similarly, this process defines your experience of the dark messages that are raining down upon you and how you handle that information determines the outcome as well. As you absorb and ingest the doomsday reports and survival menaces that have become your daily bread, your perception of those possible realities affects the actions of the dark force and their impact upon the greater whole.

You see this in the most simple situations. When those who hold power over you step too far over the line, and you rebel, they step back. The energy cannot move forward. When, instead, you bow down and allow fear to blind you, they roll over you—profiting from the momentum of your weakened will to manifest their aggression in that particular circumstance.

You do see why it is so essential to your spirit development and the orchestral sounds of the Universe that you operate in right mind, responsible for every thought and every word you utter ... and that you finally acknowledge and then dispel those shadowy forms that still lurk about in the deep waters of your soul.

Where there are no more secrets or denial, you operate in the light of absolute consciousness, clear and unfettered, and that is the foundation from which the soul climbs higher. Otherwise, what lies unresolved at the "below" of those murky waters will rust and tarnish your conscious vision of all that you create in the foreground—the "above," where all is manifest.

13

Past Lives and Simultaneous Realities

We will endeavor now to shed more light into the haze of misperception surrounding your understanding of past lives and simultaneous realities, asking you always to consider how "past" and "future" exist only as three-dimensional concepts that hold no true measure beyond the physical reality—yet we must bear in mind how very real they are to you.

That point of reference in which you have crystallized, a conjunct on the time-space continuum, we can describe as your "contemporary" Earth—2002 full journeys around your Sun from the "time" the Christed One walked amongst you—but do remember that every time we use these terms we are doing so because you are still operating in the "time" zone. Since you still relate events in linear time, we remain somewhat constrained to make reference to it in order to help you understand how it will be for you, when time and its indicators are no longer relevant to your existence as fully conscious members of the multidimensional Universe.

We ask, too, that as we progress in the discussion of parallel realities and the strings of consciousness laced throughout the no-time, you recognize and remember how every cell of your body is a dynamic universe unto itself—no less than the galaxies of celestial beings in the heavens, no less than the most complex thought of Creation.

We have spoken at length of how Spirit crystallizes as matter, consciousness vibrating out into the cosmic sea as thought— thought slowing its frequencies to resonate with the cosmometric patterns that constitute the blueprints of life emerging in the density of the physical universe.

There are now master teachers amongst you who are reviving the fundamental Sirian teachings of cosmometry (sacred geometry) and the Creator's mathematics, and their work is bringing to many a new understanding of how the patterns of consciousness are imprinted upon the cosmic sea and how life springs forward from those designs—crystals of perfect symmetry, untold intelligence, and immense beauty.

We celebrate the bright light of their vision and their commitment.

Throughout your lengthy history and countless civilizations, mystics and light beings (those in body as well as others, hovering about on the higher astral), who were committed to safe-guarding the Sacred Wisdom, have been utilizing their knowledge, abilities, and vibrations to anchor the light in your realms ... awaiting a time when the human race would be **ready** for them to appear before you.

That time, you know now, has arrived.

Those who are currently in body, the Keepers of the Records, are retreating from their snowy mountaintops and remote sanctuaries to join with you. They are leaving behind their sacred lands and isolation, in order to disseminate the knowledge that has been so diligently guarded and held secret in those sacred halls.

Their assignment at this time is to gift you, the awakening human race, with the tools that will help you reestablish the balance of earth energies, generate the electromagnetic frequencies that will tone the population back into harmony, and establish the pace of the metronome that will hold the rhythm, facilitating Gaia's passage through the great vortex.

You can understand why the Tibetans—great masters of sound and its impact within and upon the material realm—have had to abandon their sacred space, closing down the primary portal at Kailas, in order to bring to the new generations of your race their acquired knowledge of the Cosmos, the great Planet Earth, and the essence of human nature.

As Keepers of the Records, they are amongst those heart-centered leaders who will guide you through the Desert Days with a profoundly reverent understanding of the forces of the Universe, helping you all to raise consciousness and join in the chorus—the new harmonics of Gaia's rebirthing.

The earth temples of enlightenment and reverence—those raised with the dedicated hands of man; those that exist in the kingdoms of nature—are closing down because you are now enjoying direct interaction with these Record Keepers—and because a most significant aspect of the wisdom that was held in those spaces is that **nothing is permanent.** The new is being birthed all around you.

Indeed, as Gaia's shifting energies traverse those quickening vibrational waves of Ra's imminent passage, the crystalline consciousness of those walls and great altars, the great forests and the seas, is shifting, reorganizing to "materialize" in the next dimension as the liquid light of the One Heart.

In the end, you understand that all that is material will eventually de-materialize and dissolve, for the nature of the physical realm is that the theater changes constantly and with great eloquence and that the cosmometric patterns that form there rearrange themselves—reflecting the evolving consciousness that defines and designs all realities.

That which is infinite, the inner sanctum, is the mind—it is the thought, the vibration; it is the focused intent of consciousness, which creates it, the architectural blueprint of all life ... the DNA. It is the mathematics of creation—the Music of the Spheres. It is the "container" of those vibrations that have been bouncing about in its parameters, reverberating Spirit through its sacred forms and spaces, just as the light of the Universe shines through every cell of your bodies. It is the vibration itself.

It is the wheel of the Navaho; it is the Tibetan mandala—now a complex lattice of brightly-colored sands ... now a fading memory, blowing eternal in the wind.

You are always capable of accessing what you need (as is appropriate to your evolutionary pace) from deep within—where, in the perfection of your own godliness, Truth unfolds the magic of life. From within that god seed, there where the conscious thought of all creation pulsates your eternal **becoming,** you are always and constantly extracting the absolute knowledge of All That Is, That Ever Was, and That Always Will Be.

Greater numbers of you have begun to raise your antennae, so that you may receive us, light beings of other dimensions—souls just a few steps ahead of your own. So do you, in ways you will soon understand, send consciousness to those realms that have yet to know the magnificence of your stage of awareness. At the next level, whereby you move into the "fourth dimension," you become far more aware of how consciousness creates, and you will recognize your souls in action! You will be amazed at just how translucent the veil draped between these realities really is.

We are pleased to see that you who seek to balance the available esoteric teachings with a scientific foundation—a logical sense of things—have reached a heightened awareness in your study of "quantum physics." For you, the old paradigms of the nature of the Cosmos have begun to break down under the weight of the "unexplainable" phenomena that constantly occur in the Cosmos born of the Primal Thought—a limitless Universe that is constantly and eternally being co-created from all those units of consciousness that emerge from Source.

Others, who are more intuitive in their perceptions, do know and understand the workings of Spirit at the "gut" or visceral level, and that is an advantage ... but it is not a necessity.

Regardless of your approach or experience, for you who seek the Sirian perspective (overlighted by those eight-dimensional radiations that are illuminating this work), we wish to elaborate how each unit of consciousness moves in and out of various dimensional contexts.

However slowly the soul intends to progress, however rapidly it leaps forward, it follows a specific direction determined by its focused intent as it proceeds along the path of return to Source.

To contemplate how and why one enters the physical lifetime and walks as a conscious being on any given planetary station in the material universe (for it is not necessary to be earth-bound to reincarnate), or where one "goes" when (s)he exits from the physical and then returns to it is, to say the least, a curious exercise that even the most diligent seeker struggles to envision and truly comprehend.

The soul purpose of that repetitive passage upon the karmic wheel of learning and experience escapes most of those who are still working through those processes, going around and around again, like mice running blindly upon the spinning wheels of their cages. Traveling similar roads, lifetime to lifetime, appears in many ways to be an inane and futile process, and it is quite difficult to imagine that it is your soul that chooses to do so, as a necessary process of its refinement and progression.

But, of course, there is nothing futile about it—for the intricate design of the Cosmos of Soul is perfect, and everything that occurs within it serves a purpose. Despite the illusions of imperfection, such as those that we have depicted earlier on and which are part of your experience in this phase of your evolution out of *samsara,* everything that exists is absolutely integral to the unfolding of All That Is in its myriad aspects, dimensions, and expression. Even the darkness, you are learning, has its place in the great scheme of Creation.

The illusive wheel upon which your soul takes exercise is in effect a magnificent spiral, Creation imploding, moving you, as soul essence, to greater heights and eventual illumination—bringing you ever closer to the magnificence of your merging back to the Godhead.

All souls move up eventually.

The darkest ones, the brightest stars ... all return.

All return to Source.

⁘⁙⁘

Your limited ability to mentally construct a timeless reality requires that you perceive this karmic process as a sort of linear procession—a following of one lifetime in body from another in a sequence of experiences and personalities that places you at key locations in history with which you find resonance.

Some of these you recognize—others you do not.

You visit Egypt, for example, and you immediately feel an enormous connection to the markers and icons that have been left for humanity—the sacred geometry, its cosmometric under-pinnings, the vibrational layering of energies that have entered there—a compelling feeling that you know it at a very deep, personal level. You experience what you term a "past life recall" of that time and/or place, connecting with what you retrieve there as former life memories—memories brought to the surface at that time of your "returning."

There are other experiences that you cannot fathom, whereby you journey out-of-body to places that exist nowhere on your Earth—experiences of alien civilizations and strange landscapes, of other dimensions, of parallel universes. Growing numbers of you have realized that you are not from this world, but have "walked in" to experience and participate in the current earth events that are drawing so terribly much attention from other civilizations—near and far.

Those who do not intend to ascend with Gaia can and often

do experience themselves in another physical reality with which their soul has found resonance and intends to crystallize in its next incarnation—a "future lifetime," in terms that would be more easily understood in your reference.

You may, in yet another manifestation of what you call "past life recall," experience resonant thought forms in the dream state, haunted in waking that where you have gone in that altered state was a place you knew intricately. You may feel it when you look into the eyes of another—someone you instantly recognize as an old soul with whom you have shared a journey or two along the way. You may be catapulted to an all-too-familiar memory by the mere wafting of a scent, a birdsong, or someone's touch upon your shoulder.

These life-altering events are often relegated to that nebulous mind space where you store the unexplainable bits and pieces of your puzzles, until you can paste them together into one cohesive picture of reality ... as you imagine it to be. There, they are strung into a series of what you believe to be a chronology of past life experiences, for that is how most conscious beings, still restricted by the restraints of linear time, put the pieces into a working framework.

First one, then the next, then the other ... a sequence, you see, rather than an overlaying of resonant frameworks that co-exist simultaneously, interdependent, interpenetrating, and all vibrating in unison, much like crashing waves in the great oceans—much like those that just barely caress the shores of the stillest seas.

As we are committed to lifting the veil from your experience and helping you access the Secret Wisdom, which serves you now, we wish to suggest a more far-reaching interpretation (a multidimensional viewpoint) of what your soul is actually creating, from that which you most likely still perceive as your journey through this one or many hundreds of lifetimes.

As consciousness units of All That Is, you bear within the seed thought of every cell of your being a knowledge and an experience of all realities ... all dimensions. Just as every individual cell of your body, by nature of the intercommunicating network of your DNA, communicates with every other cell—so do you, by nature of the scintillating waves of consciousness permeating every layer of reality and their corresponding electromagnetic frequencies, communicate with every other being in your physical world and in worlds beyond.

That you are not necessarily aware that you do this does not negate the fact that it occurs constantly and on levels that you cannot even perceive at this time in your evolutionary development.

These other beings, of themselves the same essential elements as you (for all is one in the Cosmos), are you—and you are they. Unfortunately, at this stage of your collective awareness, there is still a pervading sense of separateness, which renders most of you incapable of perceiving (for any sustained periods of awareness) the absolute oneness of all that exists about and within you. How then can we elucidate to you how this intercommunication of consciousness creates your every reality?

Let us consider all we have shared with you regarding the progression of your thoughts and their resonant waves as they ride upon the open seas of cosmic consciousness.

In full light body, when you do not exist as a physical form, you draw upon possible realities—a sort of holographic field—

which you determine you wish to experience for whatever lessons or gifts they can offer to the expansion of your soul. These illusive "places" or "periods" or "worlds" are, in multidimensional terms, mere projections of the soul—the cosmic soul—and yet you can resonate to them, crystallize within them, and in a very illusive sense—become them.

We tax you, for you are in one such holographic reality at this very moment, and perceiving it from beyond its confines is just as difficult to you as the concept of height to the flatworm ... but it is so.

As members of the earth community, you have materialized this abstraction, in a very limited way, as television—so let us use this analogy to express the concept more clearly to you.

When you watch television or entrain yourselves with video games, whereby illusions of real-life and "virtual" people and events are played out daily on the mechanical viewing screens in your homes, you find you are drawn into the dramas that are portrayed there—those, at least, with which you find a form of resonance that can be described as an "emotion-based" symbiosis. On some level, you experience the pain and sacrifice of the heroine, the hero's grandeur, the revenge of the victimized, and all the myriad emotions enacted in such scenarios (provided for your "entertainment") as your own emotional experiences and desires.

When you watch broadcast news and react to how it is presented to you, you are easily moved to feelings of despair and hopelessness over the world situation—focusing your energies in the base chakra center and then reflecting that vibrational imbalance to others with whom you come into contact in the immediacy of your family and close contacts. That, in turn, affects the community in which you participate, lowering the consciousness of your environment.

If you are in the mood for humor and laughter, you quickly switch channels when you are served up violence and inhumanity, and only when you find that program which resonates with your state of mind do you lie back, relax, and allow yourselves to enjoy what is being enacted before you. You find resonance with that hologram, and you allow it to impact and alter your emotional, mental, and physical bodies—for laughter activates endomorphs in the body, your pleasure centers, and so the very nature of experiencing the holographic representation of a "funny" illusion resonates with your cellular components, every nerve, every element of your being.

The energy runs up the ka channels, the byways of your complex mental, physical, and spiritual bodies, and you center yourselves in the heart and throat chakras, sending out on the waves a sense of contentment and peace with the world—and this, too, is reflected in the ethers.

If that is not a god-like ability to co-create reality, then what is?

We are not saying that your experience as 3D beings in the physical universe is unreal—or that it is somehow less important than another. That is not our intention—but oh, how complex it is to observe one layer of reality from a higher perspective, when you are still constrained in its limiting parameters. This we do know, for we have experience of those passages and stages of evolution, and we, too, have strained to grasp what now we are capable of effortlessly utilizing as tools to our increasing understanding of the Cosmos of Soul.

Relating this information back to the question of past lives and parallel realities, is it possible that what you believe has been an experience of a "before" might simply be the reaching of resonance with a thought whose manifestations in the holographic world of 3D have activated a particular center of your own divine consciousness—to be made your own?

The channel asks that this information be stepped down in complexity.

A scent can transport you to a simultaneous reality because within the patterns of consciousness of that smell are vibrational frequencies upon which your minds ride, like surfers on the waves, to that alternative experience instantaneously. A sound wave can similarly strike a resonant chord within your cellular patterning that aligns every cell of your being with the frequencies that occurred in that moment—vibrations that are in tune or resonant with parallel universes in which you do also exist—and so it is that every time you hear that sound it will always transport you to that reality. It serves as the vehicle upon which you are capable of traveling to that experience, and it will be resonant to you forever.

A given lifetime, reflecting back to you all the cosmometric patterns laced through it, is as such resonant with you eternally, which is how you journey back and forth in "time," in space, across the galaxies. Not only do you journey to observe these realities—you do exist within them, and therefore you do utilize those experiences to affect new outcomes continually.

You can and do constantly alter outcomes of this lifetime (there where you have focused your consciousness at this point on the time-space continuum) by attuning to alternative "lifetimes" or "locations," experiencing the primary situation from that vibrational frequency, and applying your acquired skills and knowledge at those harmonic levels to the current or present experience.

If ever you have walked the sands of the Sahara—you still exist there, just as that "time" of Egypt still exists on other planes. And if you still exist in that framework of Egyptian consciousness, then clearly you are operating from that point in the no-time, every bit as much as you are from that which you perceive as this point—this lifetime—this reality.

And you can only derive that, hence, if you did "exist" in that holographic Egypt of your experience, then you surely were also drawing upon this "current" framework—a sort of "future" life awareness—to affect what conscious constructs and manifestations you created there ... through the wisdom and abilities that your ever-evolving soul carries through all experience.

You can call these "past" and "future" lives if that is more comfortable for you. It is closer by far to the multidimensional perspective if you can experience reality in these terms rather than in the constricted vision of a spiritless world through which you walk one time and once alone—only to die, never to exist again.

⁝⁝⁝

How you hold consciousness in parallel realities is quite remarkable, for there are any number of possibilities that souls create in the limitless Universe. Remember, you are sparks of the god-light, which means that all the tools of universal mind and its wisdom can be accessed by every single cell—each a consciousness unit—to assist you in playing out the wonder of Being.

The soul can split or fragment, in which case, as soul essence, you become attached to an experience, as if a part of you becomes frozen in the slowed frequencies of a traumatic situation or exchange and, in a sense, remains "stuck" to a memory, another being, or an environment.

The fragment of soul consciousness that separates (just as you, a spark of light, have separated from Source) is free to connect with any level of awareness or conscious being with which it finds resonance. It can break away, move into the light, experience "death" from that limited perspective, and return in a completely different embodiment, creating a rather complex state of being, which we ask you to consider as "parallel lives" within the lifetime.

There is every possibility that you have encountered that part of you in another, with whom you are so close that you recognize every note that plays between you as the music of your own song.

It is often the case that a fragment leaves and you disassociate from that aspect of your soul, forgetting it, and yet it remains corded to you—attaching you to the trauma that caused it to break away.

This can occur within the framework in which you are consciously self-aware, such as that which you perceive as this lifetime, or it can cross over to other dimensions and parallel universes. Whenever the appropriate "chord" is struck, that part of you that has remained glued to the experience—a piece of your soul—stirs, but the discord of the trauma and the waves it continues to emit through the ethers often disturb the music of the soul ... and that part of you simply can no longer find its way back.

Consider how another soul with whom you have created these

cords may have decided to digress, choosing to journey into the shadowland to understand how it created the trauma and to forgive it. Meanwhile, you remain tethered there, working through the other's experience. Imagine if a part of your being attaches to one who leaves your realm and reincarnates upon another planet or somewhere else upon the cosmic sea, a place still incomprehensible to you as a contemporary earth resident.

Imagine, too, that if another soul essence decides it wishes to journey through the Cosmos by "attachment" to you—then you can become a host for a soul-merging with another human being, extraterrestrial, or entity traveling upon the ethers.

As that one moves about in the unknown, a part of you passes there as well, and that can be intriguing—as it can be difficult. The realities created by these strings of consciousness traversing the Cosmos are endless, for the soul extensions of so many conscious "units" have no boundaries other than their own progression out of the darkness and into the light.

You can imagine what confusion can be wrought by such infinite possibilities of soul moving in and out of body, traversing endless universes, and resonating through the many dimensions of the All That Is.

⁂

Now it is time for a coming home of any fragments that have broken away or wandered off to explore of their own. It is a time for absolute integrity, for you are soon to pass through the great vortex, and you want to be whole, unfettered, and aware.

You need those parts of you that have chosen to attach to another experience, another being, or another reality to bring that knowledge back in, to nest within you—retrieving the memory and healing the injured soul.

Knowing that fragmentation occurs during traumatic and painful experiences, when the soul bleeds and wounds are formed, will help you understand that this separation is not for the highest good: not for you, not for the reality to which you have bonded, and not for the fragment.

Those parts of your soul that have separated can be called home when you are ready to reclaim them, forgiving the cause of those traumas that sent them to seek safety elsewhere.

If it is your wish to heal the soul fragments—those that have strayed, those that have corded to others—you can do so by bringing the lost pieces of your being back in, through the heart, prepared that the process may require that you confront and experience the pain or suffering that caused them to break away.

Absolute honesty with yourselves is paramount. Only you know if the time has come to call back the pieces of your soul-mind. It is your free-will choice to make, but it is going to be necessary if you intend to integrate and journey unencumbered into the bright light of your liberation.

We are here to offer you guidance—will you take our hand, to walk as giants amongst the stars?

Meditation

Calling Home the Fragments of the Soul

You will close your eyes now and take yourself to the center of your being—that place you recognize as the very core of your existence. Go deep, deep within, slowing your breath and being aware of the rhythm of your breathing.

There is a flame of light that is your very essence—you can see it as you peer into the darkness. Breathe deeply, and with each breath feel the flame expanding, its light moving upward into your head, down to your toes, and throughout your body. Let the light expand outwards, into the space that surrounds you, and inwards, filling every cell so that your entire body slowly becomes filled with light. Breathing ... feeding the flame.

As you become filled with the brilliance, send this light beyond your immediate field, reaching out to the light beings that hover around you. Call upon the warriors of light to surround this area and to act as a barrier of light against any energies that are not of the highest order and intention. Now, slowly open the crown center, extending a beam of light from your head like a beacon to the Light Ones of all Creation—asking them to connect with you. They will. They will come when you call out. Feel the oneness. Bask in it. Experience yourself as one with all the light beings of the Universe—the All That Is, That Ever Was, and That Always Will Be.

Feel the light of so many beings filling you, passing through your crown, down your spinal cord, and radiating through your heart ... moving through your body ... descending into the earth. Imagine this as a luminous cord of light running through you, weighted by a golden anchor at the base of your spine, and now send it deep, deep to the below. When you hear it hit bottom, be sure that you hook it firmly to the rocks—holding you firmly in Earth's fields.

*Within this brilliant light you can make out a form—
it is **you**. The light of your consciousness is directed by
Higher Beings and your guides to scan this form, to know
it, to look for any areas where there may be fragments or
pieces missing. This is a most important moment in your
self-awareness, a taking stock of who you are and where
you come from. Take your time, observing every part of
you, making a note of any places that seem inharmonious
or empty. There may be many . . . there may be a great
chasm or just a little fracture or hole . . . any experience is
right. Where there are many fragments, you will choose
the aspect that is the most important at this time in your
life, and you will be guided to know which one that is.*

*Call out to this missing part of you, this aspect of your
being, to come to you from wherever it has gone. It may
be very close to you, or it may have drifted away. Call out,
asking it to come to you. It can hear your call, and it will
come towards you. Send the call through your heart center.
This fragment will feel the heart calling it to come home.*

*You may be able now to see this piece. As this aspect
approaches you, does it do so with reservation . . . or does it
come to you without hesitation? It may show itself to you
in imagery or speak to you quietly. Be patient. This is
reunion, a time of rediscovery.*

You need to feel.

*Often the fragments arrive and show you a play or act out
a scene that may have completely escaped your conscious
memory. You may ask for information: Where has this
part of you been hiding? How long has it been gone? What*

caused it to stray? You may be shown an incident where it became separated from you, attaching itself to that moment—freezing itself there. Look at who else was involved . . . who else is part of that moment and place. Sometimes, a fragment leaves to protect you, and that too you are free to see now.

Take your time with this . . . you may have been separated for a very long time.

Does this fragment want to come home? You can ask. Do you want this part to come home? What have you gained by this aspect being away from you, and what have you lost?

Recognizing this part of you may not immediately heal the trauma that caused the fragment, but it is a beginning. Tell this part of yourself that you love it and want it to come home. In spite of the way you act sometimes, deep down inside you really do love this part. And perhaps more difficult—you need it. Without it, you are incomplete, and you want to be whole.

Is there anything you need to do for this part of yourself—something that would make it easier for this one to return? It can tell you if you ask. It has many, many things to teach you. Before drawing this part of yourself back into your being, ask if there is anyone else with it? If so, tell it that that one must stay behind, at least for now. Perhaps goodbyes need to be said.

Call this one back to you now, back to that place within you from whence it separated. It remembers. And when it has returned, place your arms over it, just as you would hold a child, to bring light, to bring healing and accept-

ance, as you reunite. Hold this part of you close ... letting yourself feel into it.

How does it feel to have this part of you back? It is so important to feel. It is important to remember anything you may have promised or said to this part and remember to live up to it. The wounds can be healed now, but you must keep your promises and honor this part, or it may leave again. Maybe you need to talk to this part of yourself on a regular basis. And if this part has made promises to you, you need to be sure the promises are kept.

Now, wherever this part of yourself has returned, place your hands there—if there is anything you need to say to this part of your being, take a moment to do that now. Take a deep breath—trust that the process will continue, even when your attention is elsewhere. Now call on the Angels of Light to apply light to this area to help the integration process and know that they will do what's necessary for you ... for you and for the fragment.

Slowly imagine the beam of light from your crown retracting and gently closing—like the petals of a lotus. Draw up the light from the earth as well, asking that the anchor remain with you. Soon all you can see is a tiny point of light, and then it disappears.

Bring your hands to your heart and just feel.

Breathe deeply.

And when you are ready, slowly open your eyes and bring yourself back gently—taking all the time you need to integrate what you have brought forward.

14

Death versus Ascension

To us it appears that most of you are as mystified about the process of ascension as you are about death, for both of these transitional phases of your return to Source involve your evolution out of the body and the primary reality—the "known"—however little you truly "know" about it. Both are frightening in that to contemplate either requires that you confront the ultimate secret to your current existence—a secret that only the process itself can reveal with any certainty ... and often not even then!

Aggravating your anxiety over the death process and accentuating your fear of it is a tremendous lack of understanding over what actually occurs in the passing from physical to pure spirit essence. This is exacerbated by traumatic rituals of separation when death occurs, the uncertainty of what actually awaits you on the other side, and an overwhelming fear of all that which will cause you pain, immense suffering, and the unbearable grief of separation.

Only those native beings who have remained attuned to the unfolding of spirit and the true seekers amongst you have dedicated themselves to preparation for that evolutionary process of transition: a welcoming of winter, knowing that the springtime of the soul always follows.

Similarly, your excitement over Earth's ascension and the prospects of your individual participation in that process are diminished by the ever-looming specter of global Armageddon, which interprets the imminent shifting of your favorite heavenly body as the doomsday hour for the life forms of your world. This, too, creates all manner of fear for the unenlightened and for those who are blindly unaware and totally uninterested in the celestial dynamics that are constantly redefining the "parameters" of the Universe.

Seekers of peace and the loving way, you cannot help but question why the unfolding of such ecstatic transitional events as those that have begun to manifest throughout your ascending solar system must necessarily include such violent opposition and obstruction, which you are now witnessing in the playing out of the Secret Government's dark and dangerous games.

When you are at center, feeling balanced and clear of mind, you reaffirm that it is not at all necessary and that you do not intend to fuel the dark forces by giving your power over to the collective depression, born of fear and hopelessness—emotions that so defeat the spirit.

From a place of clarity—the center of your being—you do your best work on individual and collective levels to neutralize the impact of the opposition, bringing those around you up to the light of your hope and celebration. You serve as a model for others, standing tall in your commitment to the creation of a better world for yourselves, for your families, for all the living beings of Earth—and beyond. From that place of calm and serenity, you find security in your understanding of how raising Gaia can indeed become a smoother and more joyous experience than that which is currently manifesting in the smoke and haze of those who would destroy the beauty.

You must, therefore, be clear of those shadows that evoke fear in you—and of firm resolve. This you know is accomplished by freeing the lower chakras of any blocked energies, thought forms, or entities that have nested within you, so that you can clear the ka channels and run pure pranic energy through your crowns and into the umbilical cord that grounds you to the Earth Mother.

Then will you be your most effective as lightworkers for the human race and guardians of the deity in transition, always remembering that it is a glorious Earth that you wish to ride into the fourth dimension—and the highest good of all souls, which is your objective.

We trust that you understand why we are so determined to have you stare deeply into your fear and then to dissect it, examining every piece, so that you can move it out of your way—for once and forever. Now is the time to let go of the weighty burden that "terror" creates, not only within you but throughout every conscious experience with which your mind resonates.

Indeed, this is the time to start truly rejoicing in the knowing that all that lies ahead of you is far more resplendent than that which you left behind—for you are forever moving towards the luminescence of Source, Dear Ones ... moving swiftly into the pure brilliance of Eternal Light.

The thought of relinquishing the body and those tempestuous and pleasure-filled earthly connections for the unknown is nonetheless bewildering to you—this we do understand. Further intensifying your concern and sense of insecurity is the question of how ascension will affect you personally.

Will you "make the grade"... or be cast out of Ra's embrace?

It is only natural that it remain a great mystery to you how these realities and probable outcomes are manifesting about you, what your role in these processes is to be, and (from a perfectly practical standpoint) just what lies in store for you at a very personal level.

Who will choose to experience transition, or death, when all moves through—and who will not? Is that really your choice to make now, as free-will members of the human race—or was it determined well before you entered body, at the soul level?

How do you even make the distinction between death and ascension? Will you suffer, will you celebrate ... will you even be aware of your passage?

These existential questions and concerns we, too, have pondered. We have known your same doubts, your fears, and the trouble lurking in your souls as you search to truly comprehend that secret of your immortality, which lies just beyond the portal of physical life, as you currently know it from your temporary stations in the third dimension.

So let us contemplate the essence and the meaning of existence from the greater perspective to gain a sense of our individual part and participation in the great cosmic plan.

Consider the nature of All That Is: the Source, the Monad, Universal Mind, the Eternal Flame, God.

Contrary to the myth and science of most dogmatic schools of human thought, there is no beginning to Creation—no "big bang," just as there is no end—no apocalyptic finality. Totality (the All That Is, That Ever Was, and That Always Will Be) is all encompassing, timeless, and without limitation. Any attempt to define, categorize, or contain it seems, inevitably, only to remind us of our own limited scope and capabilities.

We, evolving units of consciousness, are dwarfed by our individuality—that "I am" awareness that limits the uninitiated, in varying degrees, to a perception of distinctly separate units within a whole, rather than of the whole itself.

Each spark of the godself is a perfect replica of the totality, and within it are contained all the dimensions, every design, and all the cosmometric proportions that exist throughout every layer of reality. Thus it is that each spark is capable of the works of the Creator, for each is constantly co-creating the Cosmos.

You are that spark. You are the creator of numerous universes (just as you are the **creation** of numerous universes!), and your bodies are the manifestation of all that which is godly about you.

Death and birth co-exist as Creation within you in myriad forms and abstractions. Cells are constantly dying, so that others can be born. Certain bacteria prevent others from proliferating, holding the balance; invisible parasites who find hospitality in and upon your physical body (as well as your astral fields) carry away the debris in a perfect dance of cleansing and renewal.

There is an innate balance in all things, dying and being birthed, building and tearing away, pushing and pulling, heating up and cooling down. Consciousness crystallizes and later dissolves in the perpetuity of Being. All is operating just as Universal Mind intends; all is breathed into being and then out of being, progressing and evolving from one state to another, eternally seeking refinement.

From this Totality, the state of utter perfection and absolute consciousness that creates all existence, emerges (as part of that experience) the infinite cosmometry of universal design through which aspects of that creative force, the Entirety, form as self-aware units, sparks of the flame, entities of "I am" awareness.

This is what we intend as the "soul"—a spark of the Eternal Flame of Creation that leaps from the fire and burns its incandescent light through innumerable experiences, never to be extinguished, so that it may eventually bring back to Source that which it has created, resolved, and illuminated.

It blazes a path along the great spiral of ascension, searing its vibration into the matrix of cosmometric proportions and design—the superstrings of consciousness that traverse the body of All That Is. At the onset of that journey, when the soul plunges into the abyss, the light that shines from that infinitesimal spark is at its dimmest, and that is when and where the material realms are created.

There, in the density, is where your solar deity, Ra, currently resides, and it is from these slowed vibrations that you are rising. Such is the eventual experience of the macrocosmic beings of the Universe . . . so is it yours, as the microcosmic representation of all that scintillates in the Cosmos of Soul.

⁎⁘⁎

At this stage of your soul's progression, whereby it travels as pure consciousness upon those strings of reality, it chooses to manifest form—to crystallize—and enter a select point of entry in the material sphere.

The primordial experience, that first manifestation of a new soul taking form, is cataclysmic to the soul essence, which has no acquired experience with which to measure itself, in a reality formed of such slowed vibrations and frequencies. New souls entering the physical for the first time are stunned by the intense polarity and opposition that exist there, and they often walk boldly into the darkness, to experience it and to learn about separation in its most immense and discernible expressions.

Having no prior experience, they leap into the reality, fueling the dynamics of polar opposition, just as those older souls, who are leaving the realm forever or who are awaiting yet another spin upon the wheel of karma, bring resolution to the contrastive forces of their specific lifetimes.

You may realize that a tidal wave of new souls has been entering the Earth zone for the past two decades of earth time. Based upon what we have told you of regeneration and renewal, the reason for such an onslaught should be clear to you—but let us not take your perceptions for granted. Instead, we shall proceed to illustrate what we believe is the purpose of this extraordinary and massive soul arrival.

As Gaia prepares to leave the realm, exceptional numbers of new souls preparing to incarnate have been magnetized to enter her electromagnetic fields by the awesome polarity that is manifest in her transmuting mental, physical, and spirit bodies and by your struggle ... along with the prospects that such dynamics offer for their accelerated evolution. The waves of contrastive energies play the strings of consciousness in the Cosmos, and that dynamic tension—the fields of opportunity for evolutionary quantum leaps—resounds through the ethers.

At any given point in the unfolding Universe, the number of new souls entering is usually in perfect balance with the many who are departing. However, at the end days of an Age, such as you have known as the passing from the Piscean to the current Age of Aquarius, there tends to be an abundance of new ones coming into a given planetary realm. Such significant vibrational shifts serve as magnets for the new sparks that have embarked upon the course of individualism to pursue the incredible journey, which we refer to as the "cosmic return."

You can imagine how much more appealing is this convergence of cycles—the ending of ages coinciding with solar ascension!

Entering upon the latest soul migrations are a number of exceptional children, who we have identified as "The Violet Oversoul." Let us not create confusion. These Violets are not the new souls we have been describing to you here—rather, they are light beings who have opted to retrograde back into the Earth realm to help usher you through the maze and confusion, as the shifting sands of your stormy waters redefine humankind's understanding of the nature of all reality.

They are sentinels of the Family of Light, dedicated in service to Gaia, and you are beginning to hear of their presence amongst you. You will recognize them as they take their positions around the globe—burning the fire of their collective consciousness through the gridlines of the power and disrupting the power lines by the sheer force of that energy.

Of this brilliant iridescence, the Light of the Violet Oversoul, we will speak in greater detail in our upcoming discussions of ascension and its particular significance to those of you who will be moving up with Gaia.

You can understand why so many reincarnating souls, aliens of distant civilizations, and extradimensional beings are attracted to Earth and to the extended family of planetary beings that comprise the chakric centers of your solar logos. Dark and light teams from the reaches of the Cosmos are lining up to observe the galactic "happening" in Ra's enormous auric body. They are everywhere about you now—preparing for contact before you go through. This you are to know in short order.

Bear in mind that, although the Government still insists on keeping you uninformed about the alien civilizations that exist just outside your door, intelligent life does thrive on the other planets and moons of your solar system. The top-level echelons of the power elite know all about alien life. They are, after all, directed by the Annunaki hybrids who rule over Earth.

They have enjoyed untold favors from their alien allies, at the expense of innocent human beings and the animals that have served as the test tube species for their examinations. The secret is out—far too many animals have been mutilated and far more humans have experienced abduction to be dismissed, although the mainstream media still avoid these pressing realities in obedience to their political and corporate masters.

Other extraterrestrials, the lightworkers of other realms, are arriving from near and far to observe the cataclysmic events taking place in your quadrant. They are particularly interested in the planets Venus, Earth, Mars, Saturn, and Jupiter, as well as a number of moons where life proliferates.

Intelligent beings of your immediate galactic family—to whom we refer as the "Ra-diants," are attempting to reach you as well, but their radio signals, deemed inconclusive and worthy of almost no news coverage whatsoever, are kept relatively secret from you.

But then, have you even been listening?

Scores of Ra-diants will be ascending along with you, and they will appear to you just as beautifully as you will show yourselves to them in the unveiling—the timeless framework of the fourth dimension.

The embrace of Light Ones of many races awaits you.

What is occurring now is an extraordinary celestial event, and the opportunities being created are limitless—would you not agree?

⁂

Your shifting solar system and the stellar dynamics playing out in your quadrant of the galaxy are indeed creating innumerable probable realities that offer mass souls—old and new—the possibility to leap from the wheel of karma, transcend the trappings of the ego self and the limitations of the illusive holograms that it co-creates, and ascend with the deity into the higher states of consciousness of multidimensional mind and luminous body.

To the Family of Light, it is a magnificent homecoming ... and the anticipation of our celebration is already ringing the bells of the celestial temples.

Awareness of this sphere of potentiality provides a superb opportunity for all free-willed beings residing upon the host planets in your solar system to dramatically raise the vibration throughout Ra's body, burning through the dark clouds of your recent storms like the laser cuts steel.

Consider the density of steel, how the focused light of the laser can slice through it, and you will be reminded of the power of your focused group mind over the dark doings that are creating disharmony around you, sucking the life breath from the environment, and attempting to diminish the light that you, the lightworkers of Earth, are anchoring in your planetary fields.

Here we have an entire solar system, which has completed its commitment to the density of the realm in which it has held vibration for unthinkable measures of time (as it is marked within that framework), and it, too, has evolved to a point whereby it is ready to move up the spiral and onto another level of learning and experience.

You can imagine just what an exceptional occasion exists for those souls—new and old—who elected to enter and incarnate within this spirit body of Ra, your Sun, having selected that point upon the time-space continuum that they first determined was their pathway back to Creator.

All self-aware beings on Earth and other celestial bodies in your solar system are soon going to have the rare opportunity to take the gargantuan leap onto the next level of awareness, which we have consistently referred to as the "fourth" dimension. Others, those who are so mesmerized by the slowed vibrations of the physical body that they will choose reincarnation over ascension, will remain tethered to the illusive manifestations of consciousness as it creates in the 3D realm.

Joining those still dedicated to the acquisition of experience in the Earth realm—those still bound to the karmic wheel of reincarnation—this mass of new souls will only fleetingly partake of your planet's energies. Gaia, moving rapidly into the vortex of Ra's passage, will no longer be a planet of choice for those who are determined to remain bound to the karmic wheel of cause and effect, action and reaction, and eventual resolution of the debts accrued in that process. They will continue that process at other stations in the material universe.

The Great Planet Earth, together with the other planets, celestial bodies, and numerous moons that orbit the great star, simply will not be located in the density of the third dimension any longer.

But Gaia is eternal—and like you, she will continue to evolve most beautifully, a radiant, glorious deity, shedding the material reflection of all that she has created in a realm within which she no longer needs to repeat the lessons of such intense darkness and light.

So catch your breath, and step out of your own way ... if it is fear of such thoughts, rather than anticipation, that blocks the forward momentum you have achieved until now.

※

Let us speak now of old souls, as so many of you who are drawn to us are old and ancient journeyers, who are completing the cycle of birth and rebirth in those slowed vibrations of matter. You have come back this time not as souls focused upon their individual "I am" experience but to assist in the awakening— for you have evolved to that. You are dedicated to raising the All to greater heights by helping those who are lost and afraid, and you are openly accepting guidance from the Light Bearers who are all about you—overlighting your path.

Spirit warriors, you carry the torch of Truth, illuminating the world as you prepare for that Olympian leap, which will catapult you into the next phase of your exquisite progression, upon the breathtaking spiral of spiritual return.

Consider what magnetic attraction Earth, swinging wildly back and forth in the dark and light polarity of these days, holds for those new souls, and you will have a clearer understanding of why so many old souls (such as you) have also decided to be present in body.

Remember—you have evolved to it.

You have come in to bring Gaia back to center.

Ancient warriors, you have come to still the pendulum.

A huge wave of old souls entered after World War II, returning to form in order to bring global healing to the surviving and departed souls of those violent expressions of darkness and to lay ground for the coming Age of Aquarius. Many of you came in at high tide ... and you know who you are. You were renegades then, just as you are now, the guardians of so many secrets that are being exposed in the light of the Aquarian dawn.

You were intent upon steadying Gaia, as she shuddered and shook from the imbalances created by the rage of those who walked then, just as you faced them in the darkest hour of Atlantis and just as you are confronting those same dark warriors now—infantrymen of the Secret Government.

We believe that all self-aware beings capable of the multidimensional perspective can understand the significance of just such a moment, and we celebrate and respect you for taking upon yourselves the enormous task of serving as the indefatigable spirit warriors of Earth in transition.

It is not an easy road you have chosen.

Not an easy road at all.

You realize that you have reached that point upon your long

journey where you are ready to take a giant leap off of the karmic wheel of your perennial process of birth and rebirth. Together with the cosmic deities, you are co-creating a most rare opportunity to accentuate that completion in full consciousness of the persona through whom your total experience has manifested.

The veil, which only briefly rises in the passing phases of birth and rebirth, is lifting now and you are beginning to see through the dimensions—retrieving the memory of your own birth and of your soul purpose. You are realizing your immortality, integrating the entire experience of your passing, awakening the light body.

You are being activated, scintillating in your own brilliance and the illumination that you perceive throughout the realms. You are connecting, reaching, shining. And although you are still not fully, consciously aware of the process and what awaits you, you are convinced of your commitment to the light.

You are truly remarkable, Dear Ones.

We shine your reflection through the upper kingdoms, and all who resonate there are touched by the light of your souls.

All are touched by your beauty and strength.

Death and Ascension

Whereas the ascending will be fully aware of their process and will carry the personality aspects of the self in transition from those densely configured crystalline matrices of your current physical forms into the expansive light bodies of the higher dimensions, those unevolved souls who identify strongly with the ego self will not.

Their overriding ego identity and commitment to the illusions of the material reality vibrate at such slow frequencies that these souls will be nearly frozen in the density—like the great mammoth, buried alive in the ice fields of your evolution.

You can understand that the determination of some to hold their gaze upon the shadows and dust renders them incapable of perceiving the evolutionary events that are so dramatically altering their reality. To hold on to their illusion, they simply have to believe you, the awakening, to be delusional, foolish and dangerous ... else you upset the matrix.

Dedicated to the sensate experience and the feelings it evokes, they will cling to their residual emotions and their fascination with the animal within them and elect to continue the process of reincarnation.

As we have already indicated, these are decisions that were made before they entered body—although they are always free to change the record, should they decide to alter the original plan and devote themselves to Spirit. Those who do not will experience death, the passing from matter into bodiless form, in order to continue their progression at the pace that they set ... as ships sail to the rhythms of the open seas.

At that time in their transition, they may proceed to the lower astral "layer," hovering in the vibrations of this lifetime, or progress to the middle astral spiritual realm, once they have passed through the portal.

There, on the Middle Astral, they will be met by their guides, who will assist them in developing the schematic of their life plan for the next incarnation, a time of structuring and organization, wherein the assisted souls will prepare the way for other "lifetimes" of karmic potentialities and lessons.

They can elect to spend time in the Halls of Learning, to rest, or to crystallize immediately into another physical form ... forgetting who they are, forgetting their origins, forgetting all that came before.

Detailed plans will be prepared for the next submergence into the physical realm (one which most closely resonates with the vibrational frequencies of Planet Earth). The crystalline patterns of the soul's reemergence through the new mother will be determined from the resonant DNA of the selected parenting incarnates, and all will be recorded in the soul-mind, to be accessed by the higher self at varying intervals in the life experience.

Let us now consider the soul's progression from death to rebirth.

When it is ready, and all has been prepared for the new life, the soul prepares the dynamics of that conscious crystallization as focused intent to enter the physical and take form. It awaits the flicker that lights the Gossamer Web of Light when conception of the pre-selected sperm and egg takes place—and it bonds instantaneously to that moment, to be nested in the warmth of the mother. It gestates and passes through the birth canal to acquire ego-consciousness, a personality, and all the experiences that create the environments the soul set into the plan before entering.

Soon after emergence, the conditioning of infancy (initiated by those pre-natal impulses received in the womb) ground the newly entered soul in the illusions that it has selected for that particular lifetime. The veil once again cloaks the soul-mind of all prior experience, with only shimmerings of recall for those who desire and eventually train for the opening of the third eye. The struggles and joys of the sensate experience and all the karmic relationships that were created upon that spinning wheel are then continued, in other forms and varying intensities, in other holographic playgrounds in the schools of their choosing.

And now consider ascension, whereby you recognize that you are leaping off the wheel, fully aware, like suddenly stepping out of the densest dark grey fog and into the light of day—a light you had only envisioned in your dreams. The veil, which would have cloaked the memory of all that you experienced there, no longer distorts the vision. You walk boldly into the light, dazzled by its radiant splendor, sensing that you have come out of a place to which you need never return again.

In this new "dimension" into which you will have soon ascended, you can look upon that blanket of fog and recognize the many different places that exist within it: places where you have walked, places where you have focused much energy and consciousness. Here and there a tall tree stands, marking your passage, and although most of the way is blanketed by the cloud cover, you know it. You know you have been dedicated to that forest, and that the tree has been of great significance to you.

From your viewing station in four-dimensional reality, you will realize you are at the vantage point where you can observe the entirety of that realm, and you can identify places where you "existed" within it: the tree; a special place you sense just by its scent; the rainbow colors that hover ... there where you know you have been; a tower in which you have lived; a mountaintop, whose peaks you have only contemplated from the lowlands of your experience.

You look back upon that world and realize that your emergence from these familiar points of your passage has been a long time in coming. You can only be surprised to finally receive validation of whatever multidimensional awareness you had achieved before your passing: that there is nothing linear about your karmic return, one lifetime after another.

Finally, you recognize how each passing is more like diving into a yet unexplored corner of one great lake, which you can also enter from countless other access points, along its limitless shoreline and craggy cliffs. No longer are you unaware of how the oscillations of your entry and presence there ripple and resonate forever in those waters, imprinting your vibrations throughout and, in so doing, allowing you eternal access whenever you wish or need to reexperience the sensations and the challenges that the lake—at times peaceful and serene, at times dark and dangerous—provides you.

Once you have stepped into the full light of dawn, you will know just what a monumental leap it has been—a knowing that there need be no more repetition of old lessons. Imagine how you will look upon the fear and doubts of these, the Desert Days, smiling eternal in the grace of your luminescence.

For Ra, the ascending deity, that clouded realm is the nebula of the Milky Way Galaxy, where wondrous things have been achieved and acquired in the enormity of his participation in the physical universe—but from where he now emerges. Here, too, the soul of the solar logos will soon be capable of looking back upon those markers of its existence in dense matter, recognizing the vibrations held there ... as do you, when you gaze back upon the fog-covered landscape. Here, too, is the realization of one's existence—not as the single-most brilliant fire in space, but as a spark of the Infinite Light—brought to full consciousness.

This, Dear Ones, is the magnificence with which the ascending of all realms recognize that they have finally and most valiantly achieved the initiation their own souls set before them.

As you emerge from the clouded vision into light-body consciousness, you will recognize more and more clearly that what you have until now perceived as "past lives" and memories are actually very much simultaneous to where you are now and with where you are headed. You can see them, "places" there in the soup of matter that show themselves to you as memories but which you realize are simply co-existent states of being with which you hold resonance and interact.

Soon you will realize fully that what you currently believe to be past life memory is, in actuality, the mind's exquisite capacity to recognize a harmonious "space" upon the strings of super-consciousness, which play the major chords of the Universe, and its ability to play the same chords from the music of the soul.

It is not unlike the musical training of an operatic singer or vocalist, who must reproduce a specific musical note when the pianist hits the proper key. In that moment, the mind instructs the vocal cords to vibrate at that same frequency, stimulating the throat chakra "engines" to perform that task and then producing the resonant note.

Every cell of your being so plays its instrument, the DNA helix, in order to sing the music your mind is creating within you and manifesting as sound across the "wires" of the material realm … into the ethers of parallel universes.

Imagine that "notes" exist throughout the Cosmos—for the

Entirety is an enormous symphony, notes upon notes, chords, harmonies—the Music of the Spheres. You are the note, playing your music to the Maestro as "(s)he" directs the symphony, the sum total of all the parts—which you know as well—for within those superb orchestrations you play yourselves into being.

You know the music of the soul.

And so it is that whether your song reverberates dull and lusterless on the dampers of the fog-shrouded soul or whether it rings heavenly, as sweet as wind chimes in the breeze . . . your music is eternal.

Children of the Universe, your gentle souls are on their way.

Crawling upon innocent hands and knees or leaping, conscious and bold . . . your souls are heading home.

15

DNA and the Crystalline Waters of Your Being

Humankind has reached that point in its advancing awareness of the genetic formulas of life whereby the race is now capable of altering the supreme mathematics of the Creator to reconstruct the primordial patterns of biological substance. You are relearning (or more precisely, you are **remembering**) the knowledge of the late Atlanteans, handed down to countless societies over the score of human experience, with which you are capable of designing and restructuring beings of all proportions—from the minutia of molecular units to the biological complexity of your own species or that of alien seed—into new hybrid forms and mutations.

The Maya, the Egyptians, and countless other civilizations breaching the expanse of your written and unwritten history have accessed this information, as you are now. In essence, you are experiencing and bringing into the foreground of human knowledge that godly wisdom with which Creation formulates, constructs, and then builds even further upon the cosmometry of its own design.

Most progressive civilizations eventually reach this stage in their evolution, for, as gods in their own right, all intelligent members of those societies that traverse the furthest corners of the material universe are ultimately compelled to rediscover the secrets of their individual existence, as well as the workings of the greater whole—the Cosmos of Soul.

Unfortunately, the magnificence of such potential in the hands of the human race is being diminished by materialistic man's arrogant denial of Spirit and aborted through his irreverent application of genetic technology—some of which you are being sold to believe serves for the survival and advancement of your race ... and much of which is being utilized in secret by the designers of covert technologies, biological warfare, and humanoid-robotics, soon to appear amongst you.

Where there is balance, a reverence for the perfection of the Divine Plan prevents the destructive force from taking that most important of discoveries to its dark vibration—where grotesque manipulation of the genetic codes embedded in the DNA upsets the harmonies of the living and lowers the celestial vibrations of universal mind. Where there is not balance (as is the case in your own evolutionary schematic as primary residents of Earth), untold disruption in planetary harmonics sound the discord through every level and every resonant realm.

This you are witnessing now, as your journey through the Desert Days takes you to the fringes of sanity, and where the blatant destruction of the splendid Garden of Eden burns your imprint upon the immortal soul of Gaia.

Well you can imagine how thin is the grey line between "being" gods, co-creators of the Universe, and "playing" God with the principles of Creation. Indeed, that fine distinction is surely a most profound philosophical thread upon which great debate and theosophical considerations may be duly based—one with which you may sew new "empirical clothes" for your contemporary societies.

Our Elders and their team of genetic technicians learned how very fine that line of distinction was, and the implications of having crossed it, from the karma they created for Sirius and other alien worlds, for the results of the Great Experiment that unfolded on Earth wove our lowered vibration into the karmic designs and soul patterns of the starseeded human race.

Whereas those of the higher dimensions (the Alliance formed of Angel Warriors, the Andromeda Network, Ascended Masters, luminaries from the seventh, eighth, and ninth dimensions, Sirian Elders, and Pleiadian Light Emissaries) were toning light frequencies into the crystalline waters of your DNA matrix, the others, such as the Engan, were primarily committed to the biochemical aspects of your seed—the genetic drivers of their race—for it was the survival of their species that was their focus.

However their genetic imprint would be modified in the New World, their species would live on in the starseed generations.

It was their need to escape extinction, a truly three-dimensional perspective, that was their intention from the start, and that was indeed a necessary element for the seeding. Unfortunately, that fear-based consciousness (the polar aspect of the positive survival consciousness you needed to flourish in the wilds of the Earth) was also imprinted within you from the beginning.

When the grid was placed around you, deactivating ten light-coded strands of DNA, the fundamental weaknesses of all four master strains became far more prominent aspects of the human experience. From that moment on, you became entangled in a struggle between the lower and higher vibrations of your genetic "memory," and then deactivated by the base frequencies of Annunaki electromagnetic fields.

Stunned, you were trapped, so soon after your incubation, in their powerful nets—and there you have remained, until now, when (despite their desperate attempts to reweave it) the net is disintegrating in the brilliance that pours forth from the ascending soul essence of Ra.

The mistake of the Sirian Elders, just as significant, was draped in the subtle folds that form the fabric of unresolved ego consciousness, where one forgets—if even fleetingly—that any sense of omniscience distorts the clarity of the original intention and ties the intender to its mutated manifestation, creating complex karmic bonds that are all-too-often unyielding and difficult to release.

In their zeal to bring the brilliance to form and send great waves of light and love coursing through your three-dimensional universe, our Elders grossly underestimated the ultimate impact the truest intent has upon the manifestation of events in the no-time and how it determines not only the crystallization of matter in the physical reality but also its evolution within the body of Divinity.

Having inherited the legacy of those hard-earned lessons, we have consistently driven home to you the need to be in center and to always set your sights upon the highest of intentions—that the All be served—in every aspect of your existence ... and in your dedication to serve as warriors of light, healers and guides. This is of the utmost significance not only to your individual experience, or for the healing of Gaia, but for the soul patterns of the entire race ... and outward, reverberating eternally and without limitation through the dimensions and across the no-time.

No universal law denies you the right to extend yourselves, reaching for that godly experience of altering matter. Indeed, that is every bit a part of your spiritual climb as is your desire to know Prime Creator and to understand the significance of all that exists everywhere around you. Know, however, that the realization of that quest will never be successfully achieved in the tube and petri dish, the laboratory or operating room, where sovereignty is invaded—the soul essence being of no consequence or consideration—and where the sterility of the experimenter's mind is paramount to an "objective" outcome.

Rather, as we have shared with you throughout these works, the process of altering matter (disguised in the secret teachings of ancients as the "transmutation of lead into gold") is that exquisite transformation whereby heart-centered thought reaches resonance with the conscious vibration of matter, and then (through the focused intention that the highest good be served) the substance, raised to its exalted state of being, is either transmuted into new forms or disappears entirely!

The ultimate expression of your godliness occurs every time you raise the vibration of your own thoughts, those of the collective and matter of all densities and structures. Or when you simply come up to the perfection that is manifest in all the beauty that surrounds you: attuning to the scent of the rose, traveling the trill of the birdsong, journeying the rainbow bridge.

In those moments of supreme awareness, you are not merely "playing at" being godly. **You are gods,** gods of the earth kingdom, gods of the Universe, breathing your souls into the matrix, just as we have breathed into yours ... just as Supreme Being breathes the All That Is into being.

.·.·.·.·.

The unbridled fervor of your genetic scientists and technicians to dissect and then rebuild the genome of every living being reflects the duality that prevails in your highly polarized world. On the one hand, your recognition of the mathematical foundations of chemistry and biology, Prime Creator's language, is the Secret Wisdom coming to light within you—Noble Man rising to his innate gifts and intelligence. On the other, the desire of some to use the knowledge to bend reality in such ways that your race intervenes with the natural process, manipulating life and distorting it for any other purpose than the highest good of the All, is a reflection of humankind's ignorance ... shiny and dark, like polished black onyx.

That is why it is so absolutely relevant that you, the awakening, become acutely aware of the architecture of life, the DNA, and the naturally occurring mutations that are beginning to manifest within the living of all planetary systems in Ra's embrace (for life does indeed proliferate upon other planets in your solar system), just as you are wise to investigate and consider the implications of the work that is taking place in the laboratories of dark design.

Fortunately, there exists a parallel scientific community, which is just as dedicated to understanding how spirit permeates and creates every aspect of reality, and it is uniting spirit and science in a way such that both intuitives and logic-based thinkers can embrace the wisdom that emerges from its discoveries. As these free scientists—the quantum physicists—bring forward the new paradigms of your 3D reality and the multidimensional Universe, more of you are capable of conceptually recognizing the true nature of all reality.

You are beginning to realize with what splendor and intricate cosmometry the intelligence of Creation—manifesting your soul intention and the genetic continuum of your inherited families, species, and race (and starseeded ancestry)—meticulously creates your physical forms. It is coded into the very fiber of your beings: human DNA. From the etheric essence to the densest aspects of your earthly bodies (if dense they can truly be defined), all is blueprinted with a most unfathomable precision, a superbly orchestrated numerical rhythm, and cosmometric proportion.

There are, as well, controlled genetic scientists who are funded and directed by the Power to unknowingly serve the Annunaki's plan for absolute dominion over the human race. Some, assigned the daunting task of cataloguing and preserving the DNA of all living earth forms, believe they are working for the good of humankind and the protection of other species, unaware that their dedicated life's work only receives government subsidies and financing to assure that the seed of all earth biology be transported to another host planet and to the moon station—the "holding zone" of the power elite.

Others, of a far darker persuasion, are willing specimen collectors for the Annunaki and their alien collaborators, who are ever intent upon gestating a perfected slave force for other worlds, in other space and time frameworks. Some of these government scientists are serving as laboratory assistants to the Zeta Reticulans, in that phase of their invasion of human sovereignty that involves collection of human sperm and ova from unwilling and terrified "abductees"—a program intent upon saving their own devolving race from extinction.

Others still, focused upon untold economic rewards, are at work "capitalizing" on the incredible stores of wisdom contained within the designs of Creation by seeking to create and perfect biomolecular DNA computer units that are so miniscule that they can fit, a trillion at a time, into a laboratory test tube.

The potential output capacity of a microscopic DNA computer (already past the preliminary stages of its biotechnological development) is the performance of well over sixty billion controlled computer operations per second. This, the command-triggered robotization of your innate intelligence from the molecular level of your human experience, is the cutting edge of their covert technology.

One cubic centimeter of your sophisticated DNA, in its limited expression—the double helix—can store more data than all that which can be recorded and stored on over nine hundred billion compact disks of your current data management technology. As you can well imagine, that is some highly exciting information for technology designers, who are intent upon computerizing human beings.

Each live cell, container of the DNA data management molecules, is being studied for its amazing capacities to manage and code unfathomable quantities of information. The double helix molecule, foundation of your existing DNA, records data based on four primary chemical platforms—currently identified by your scientists with the scripted letters: A, T, C, and G. This provides a monumental capacity for memory and a formula that can be developed into a most sophisticated biotechnological "language"—the likes of which the gene computer technicians have only begun to tap.

Their vision of living cells serving as complex biotechnological computers that can be programmed and commanded to function as information distribution networks represents the early stages of a left-brained approach to what we are intent upon helping you access from a right-brained experience … the capacity of human awareness and focused mind to affect every molecular unit in the body, altering the make-up of the body, mind, and spirit.

Imagine … if you can … what twelve interactive DNA strands (four perfectly interfacing tetrahedrons of light) will be capable of computing? Imagine what the "junk" they told you had no recognizable function or purpose will be able to tell you, to create, to remember?

Imagine your enormous capacity, *Homo sapiens*.

And imagine, just imagine, with what majesty and light you were born into the Earth realm.

It is our intention to elaborate, in depth, the patterns of your evolving cellular consciousness and the light-encoded DNA that is operating now or lies dormant, awaiting reconnection, so that you can understand most succinctly what will occur as you rebundle these light filaments: first creating triangulation, then the star tetrahedron, the Supraluminescence, and then the perfected cosmometrical Vortex of Light within every cell of your awakened light bodies.

Before we endeavor to describe the function of the ten dormant strands of your light-coded DNA and the process of their reactivation, we must give due thought and consideration to the consciousness of the water element within your bodies and its photo/phonic transmitting capacity.

Consider that about seventy-five percent of Gaia's celestial body is water, as is yours, and know that all that which we will bring forward in regard to your own beings, microcosms of the planetary form, is absolutely applicable to the macrocosm. Water is the measure of life feasibility on your planet and throughout the material universe (in varying degrees). Without it, you and most of the animal and plant forms that inhabit Earth would be unable to maintain form in physical reality.

Like the great waves in your oceans, your fluctuating body fluids affect your internal weather and climate—the body temperature, which regulates any number of functions determining the good health of your organism. Your water stores hydrate, cleanse and purify, oxygenate, enable complex chemical reactions, distribute nutrients, affect metabolic activity, detoxify, and play host to countless organisms ... just as the great oceans of Gaia metabolize the abundant life within them.

The body water's ultimate performance, however, is to serve as a highly conductive transmitting medium for the DNA, sending and receiving electromagnetic frequencies of sound and light that are constantly being communicated from the double helix highways to cells, tissues, and organs of your bodies. Indeed, we read ninety percent of the water within you exists in relationship to the function of your DNA, primarily as a resonance factor for the communication of sound and light transmissions through the cells, between the cells, and everywhere in between.

From a metaphysical perspective, the water of your complex

physical beings is the receptive element—the cosmic sea—upon which all etheric imprints of consciousness are stored and amplified, serving as a matrix upon which every conscious and subconscious thought is organized in resonant patterns that form the cosmometry of your persona. That persona, clearly, is the reflection of the greater whole, of which each of you is a unit of global and universal design.

Now the question arises regarding the consciousness of the waters within you, which (like your earthly seas) become polluted with dissonant thought patterns, invading acoustic and electromagnetic frequencies, toxic elements from your water and food supply, and every other aspect of discord that you create on the mental level and bring to manifestation in the realm of the physical. The essential water of your make-up reflects these disharmonies, and by nature of our discussion of the conductive properties of water, it is safe to deduce that these same disharmonies are then transmitted throughout the entire organism.

Similarly, water that has been raised to resonate at its highest levels of consciousness, enhanced by your intention, water that has been purified with sound and light before you introduce it into the body seas ... water that has been thanked, loved, and appreciated will effectively communicate that higher dimensionality throughout the body.

The elemental spirit essences of water, those the metaphysicians refer to as the "Undines," respond to your conscious thoughts and then transform the essence of the water, either by slowing or raising the vibratory capacity of the element, to resonate with your thoughts and intentions.

Although we are likely to arouse dissent from the community

of health and well-being, we affirm that it is far more beneficial for you to drink tap water that has been addressed consciously and aligned through toning, sacred music, and heart-centered communication with the elemental energies of water, than it is to ingest expensive "purified" water that you drink, unconsciously, without ever considering or connecting to the life force within it.

Ideally, if your heightened awareness of the significance of water draws you to purchase excellent purified water (from which many chemical additives and dangerous trace metals have been removed) and then address the consciousness and the spirit of the element, you will have accelerated not only improved health and well-being. You will also have facilitated the heightened ability of your existing DNA to transmit operating instructions to the body and prepared the way for the integration of the third strand to be woven into the matrix.

Bear in mind what we have told you, in *The Cosmos of Soul,* regarding the Tibetans' abilities to move sound through sacred form to achieve a specific outcome, or manifestation, on material planes. Consider how harmonic frequencies affect and alter the consciousness of water and how that attuned water then affects the DNA's ability to communicate and transmit the intelligence contained within it.

Your rapidly vibrating higher thoughts, the brilliant light waves that emanate from your hearts, the exquisite frequencies produced when you play Tibetan bowls or wind chimes, the angelic music of the Ones—Mozart, Bach, and Beethoven—all harmonic frequencies introduced into the drinking water and then reflected through the body waters can potentially transform the water molecules of your being into perfected cosmo-metrical structures that embody the primordial wisdom of the Universe.

These sacred formations take form, like snowflakes, as end-less variations of the six-sided star, the hexagon—the symbol of that quintessential consideration of all existence:

> *As above, so below*
> *and*
> *as below, so above.*

No matter how discordant and energetically shattered are the water molecules of your environmentally bombarded bodies, it is the nature of life and consciousness to eventually achieve per-fection—to climb the spiral, seeking full illumination. So is every molecule of your being intent upon that soul purpose from which it was designed—to reclaim the pattern of cosmometrical pro-portion and beauty and to resonate that vibration through the Universe of Being.

Whether you are determined to consciously effect change at the cellular level or whether you choose to ignore the spiritual nature of your molecular composition, we ask that you always bear in mind that every unit of consciousness (from the sub-atomic particle to the galaxy ... to the most expansive of uni-verses that exist in the Cosmos of Soul) strives for greatness. Each beats with its own rhythm ... each is a divine product of the envi-ronment and the supreme consciousness that permeate its inner and outer space.

To ignore the consciousness of every single cell is to relinquish your ability to command these micro-units of your being to perform in perfect harmony, to create excellent health of body, mind, and spirit, and to alter any dysfunction that has occurred in your process of living in the often conflict-ridden and disturbing times through which you are now passing in body.

Indeed, ignoring that the cell is a receptive unit of the body electric means that you are utterly unaware of your own make-up and of the power that you have over all aspects of your physical manifestation.

The receptive quality of a cosmometrically aligned hexagonal water molecule is identified in the molecule's capacity to reverberate at those specific resonant frequencies that create the ideal vibrational field into which the third strand of DNA, the first etheric strand to be reintegrated into the double helix, can be eventually crystallized and ultimately anchored as a material reality—first at the molecular level of awareness, then at the cellular level, and so on.

The integration of the third strand is the most important progression of all that will follow, for it weaves into your essence the consciousness of all the celestial bodies of your solar system, the intent of the extradimensional beings who served you at the seeding, and the higher consciousness of your souls—creating *triangulation* within every cell of your being. Correctly executed, the process of the stranding instantaneously activates the thymus—the master gland and central control tower of your light bodies—like the flick of a wall switch floods a dark room with light.

As many of you are acknowledging to us in your altered states, dreams, and direct communications, this can be a most incredible experience, and often, when that flood of light courses through you, it can be quite overpowering. This is why we are concerned that you have proper guidance and preparation if and when you choose to consciously initiate the activation.

There is growing awareness of this process in those of you who are now awakening on Planet Earth, just as there is significant misinformation and a spreading of confusion as to its unfolding manifestation and its meaning to you as individuals … and to the whole of humanity.

We are aware of how distortion of this aspect of your ascension is being created and manipulated by individuals who are not grounded in unconditional love and ego-less service. We hear you calling out, asking for guidance and clarity so that you may wade through the conflictual information that is now available to you … and we wish to answer the call with the insights you need to move forward in absolute integrity, clarity of mind, and a clear focus.

As we are cautious not to interfere with your free-will experience, we will address only what we know of this process, and it will be up to you to determine who are the present earth guides whose assistance will help you accelerate your preparation … and who are not.

There are now significant numbers of lightworkers on assignment amongst you, whose genetic "rewiring" has plugged them back in to their galactic circuitry—reconnecting them to their respective star systems. As you can well imagine, this has everything to do with why they are serving as transmitting instruments, capable of attuning to and holding the frequencies that enable them to bring through extraterrestrial and extra-dimensional communications from the Family of Light.

Some (but not all) of these channels have been commissioned

to facilitate integration of the DNA material, bringing great numbers of you to triangulation. Trydjya, our primary earth instrument, has been given this assignment, and she has been instructed to prepare 144,000 first-wave ascension team members to perform that same function, which she is achieving as our representative and human voice.

A great many of you knew that you were being called to these teachings to prepare you for that experience. You may have integrated your connection with this material as a new vibration washing through you, a quite discernible physical experience, and you know without a doubt that you are being activated to that station. More of you are reporting a feeling of connection, a rekindling of some dormant memory, and that, too, is a clear manifestation of the activation that is beginning to occur within you.

Isn't it a wondrous experience, the way we have found each other ... the ways we are finding in which to unite and reconnect the "wires"? We are here for you now as the most humble servants ... as you are humble before us—for we are all light bearers committed to the godly process of soul reaching higher.

Isn't ours a most remarkable journey?

Indeed it is, Dear Ones ... indeed it is.

There are others positioned to serve in this capacity, also on assignment from light beings of other dimensions. These spirit leaders you will know not only by how their message stirs you to recognize the universal truth which they guide you to access from within—the higher self. You will also receive confirmation through recognition of their unshakable humility, their heart-centered focus, and their commitment to service above all personal gain and advantage.

If these criteria are not present and your inner guidance perceives ego-centeredness or unresolved power issues manifest in the individual, however captivating (s)he may be in the role of guide and teacher, then you are working with an illusionist— so be wary. Be discerning of all that which is coming into your awareness at this pivotal time of your expanding awareness.

Those who are working in the true light of Spirit do not want your worship, do not seek power over you, and will not accept your adoration. They are fully aware that they are not the source—they are merely the antennae, serving the dual function of receiving and transmitting energies and information. They will remind you of that throughout their teachings and healing, never allowing the ego to step in between you and the brilliance that is being facilitated through the work that, together, you have set out to accomplish. They will direct you inward, where the light of your exquisite being will shine back the wonder and the glory of all that you are discovering through your unity and mutually enriching experience.

They will celebrate your gifts, your wisdom, and your beauty … never glorifying their own.

Remember that no matter how hypnotically the glittering light of the magician appears to flicker and burn before you, the steady flame of your soul is always brighter than the dancing shadow. Learn to be trusting of the optimum guidance that emanates from within, warmed in the fire of your clear focus and free will, and you will be guided to whomever it is you are meant to find at this long-awaited point of your journey.

Many false gurus and wizards amongst you now purport to bring you to full twelve-strand awareness overnight, via various techniques and methodologies. Although we do not deny that all is possible to you as co-creators of the great shift in Ra's consciousness, we still do not perceive that as a probable reality for you at this point of the deity's awakening.

It will reach its potential when you are at that point on the time-space continuum where you have moved just within the inner orbit of the vortex center and moments from passing through—so do not delude yourselves with ego-centered imaginings now, only to be disappointed and confused later ... when nothing "extraordinary" happens, after you have invested time and energy in such pursuits as leaping from the limitations of your double-stranded DNA to the uncontainable light of the twelve.

We are telling you that, for most of you, the awakening and the seeking, the cosmic vibrations now washing over and through you are affecting the waters, raising your consciousness, and preparing you for integration of the third strand—the most significant, for it is the foundational cosmometry of what will follow, once you have achieved and anchored triangulation of the DNA.

There are very few human beings—very few indeed—whose spiritual progression is so advanced in this phase of their soul journey that they are experiencing reassembly of the secondary triangulation. And there are no human beings walking amongst you (other than the Children of the Violet Oversoul) who are currently capable of holding more than six strands ... so do not be mesmerized by those who would have you believing such overstated claims for their own edification.

The crystallization of the third strand, which you will experience (if you have not already) as an enormous leap in your multidimensional awareness, is not an immediate process. The work you are undertaking to anchor the strand requires that the frequencies you access—through the teachings of higher dimensional beings, the work of DNA activation, and the mere being in the cosmic flow now passing through Gaia—bring you to resonance with those higher vibrations and **hold you there.**

The raised vibrational frequencies of the primary triangulation of your DNA are of a clearly different nature and intensity than those of the active double helix (as it has been operative until now), and the adjustments can be extremely difficult to anchor ... just as it can be so effortless and unconscious for some that they may not even realize when the shift occurs. The experience varies from one individual to another—so much so that there cannot be a fixed description that will be relevant to the entirety, other than the very strong sensation that the polarity of your consciousness is coming to resolution and you find you are centered in Truth.

At the cellular level, incredible dynamics will be occurring as the metabolic function, having achieved the wholeness that is manifest through the balanced structure of the triad, improves dramatically—rejuvenating the expression of your being in form. So very much depends on your preparation, your awareness, and the karma that you have accumulated on your way to this point on the time-space continuum.

What is of the utmost importance now is that, in your excitement of what is unfolding before you, you maintain a self-evaluating skepticism of any desire for instant gratification—for that is the ego preening and we assure you that the unresolved ego will shut you down. We trust that we have brought that "home" to you through the telling, over and over again, of our inherited experience ... for ego-consciousness there was indeed in the design of the Great Experiment, laced through the collective of beings who willed you into being. That is a most definitive reason why the Starseed Project was not realized in full color, as the dream of the Elders envisioned it.

While you are still focused upon the **phenomenon** of your experience, your abilities, and your heightened awareness, you shut down spiritually. While you are concerned about how quickly you progress or how far along the path you have journeyed, impatiently awaiting the leaps and bounds of that process, you are moving more slowly than ever! While you are contemplating "how many" strands you have reacquired and whether or not you will be an "ascender," trust that the trickster ego self has created road blocks for the soul, and that you are possibly not moving forward as you would like to believe.

Dear Ones, please hear this message: any ego-based experience of the stranding, whereby you are focused more upon the phenomenon and its manifestation than your responsibility to serve the good of the All, will be laced with illusion and self-deceit. You will lose much spiritual ground if you yield to the ego, so be diligent. The inflated ego is the "bull's eye" for those disruptive forces that will target you, so that they can shut you down and dim the light that radiates from you.

We reiterate: some of you, who are currently accelerating this process with the master facilitators, will choose to lead others through the procedure as the first-wave ascension teams, so that you can assist the second wave to process and integrate the third strand. Required of you will be your absolute integrity and a superb capacity to remain grounded in earthly vibrations, while pulling in the celestial harmonics that will operate through you.

You will know who you are, children of the Universe.

You will know what you are to do, and how you are meant to do it.

Know that you are racing towards the New Dawn—which is inevitable, as your solar deity, Ra, prepares the way of ascension. Walk in Truth, stepping gently through your paces, allowing yourselves to be guided only where the Highest Purpose is being served for you—and for those for whom you, in turn, will shine the new light of your heightened understanding and Radiant hearts.

16

Four Times Trinity

The harmonics of the heightened cellular communication manifesting with the integration of the third strand (forming triangulation in the entire network of your intelligence communities of DNA and cellular units) creates within your microcosmic bodies a universal vibrational "template" of intelligent light coding. Around this cardinal matrix, the remaining three triad formations of etheric DNA will coalesce in three succinct stages of your passage, which you will experience as immeasurable leaps in consciousness and your progressive release from the entrainment of all three-dimensional illusion—freeing you from the grip with which it holds you locked in the polarities of your journey through the Desert Days of Earth's transition.

Illuminating every magnificent stage of your adjustment to these shifting realities, the activated pineal gland (resulting from the successful integration of the third strand), will serve as the guiding light of your souls, in a metaphorical sense, for the rest of your earth-centered journey . . . and beyond.

The pineal gland, the "control tower" of your light networks, is situated just beneath the brain matter in that part referred to as the "third ventricle"—below the cerebrum and forward of the cerebellum. It is linked to the brain through a complex switchboard of nerve connection "wires," many of which terminate in the hypothalamus (a section of the physical brain), which—united with the pituitary gland—acts as the regulator of the entire endocrine system.

Those of you who serve as healers and alternative health care practitioners are trained to understand how the endocrine system, consisting of glands that correspond directly to the primary chakras, secrete and regulate the hormones of the body, which pass directly into the bloodstream. The role of these hormonal secretions is to bring the necessary chemical "messages" to the target cells, organs, and body tissues that facilitate all the body functions required for the healthy activity, growth, and proper nutrition of the biological and spiritual being.

If you are not yet aware of these interrelating aspects of body, mind, and spirit, you may wish to take note of these connections and investigate further, providing yourselves a better understanding of how the chakric system creates, at the auric and etheric levels, that which is represented at the biological and physical levels through the endocrine system. They are the following:

The Sahasraja	crown chakra	pineal gland
The Ajna	third eye chakra	pituitary gland
The Vishuddha	throat chakra	thyroid and parathyroids
The Anahata	heart chakra	thymus
The Manipura	solar plexus chakra	Islets of Langerhans
The Swadhistana	sacral chakra	adrenals
The Muladhara	base chakra	the gonads

Very little clinical information regarding the true function of the pineal gland, understood to be linked primarily to the endocrine system, is available to the medical and scientific communities of earth biologists, who have yet to recognize its greater significance and higher purpose. It is believed that the gland is involved with the rhythms of intercellular communication, influencing the hypothalamus, but just how it functions is still a relative mystery to those who purport to be "authorities" on human physiology.

Their limited understanding is due, in large part, to the yet undiscovered fact that the pineal exists primarily as a relay station for your full twelve-stranded DNA complex—which the medical establishment has yet to seek out or discover. Although they do acknowledge the existence of that ubiquitous collection of material known as the "junk DNA," the earth biologists simply haven't uncovered the secrets surrounding the unplugging of human DNA and how the scattered puzzle pieces actually fit together.

The few who do begin to unveil those secrets are mysteriously "eliminated"—in one way or another—when they get too close to knowing or disclosing the truth of your unlimited potential, for the Power has no intention of allowing free thinkers to help you break the leaded chains of your obedience and fly, as free-willed spirits, past the boundaries of their imposed controls ... up into the clear skies of your long-awaited liberation.

Neither do they have any intention of ever revealing the secrets or admitting the lies that have for so long hidden from you the truth of your exquisite bio-spiritual nature and galactic ancestry.

It is highly unlikely that you will see, any time soon, the medical profession or the teams of government-funded biogenetic technologists embracing anything as controversial as our basic premise in regards to your genetic puzzle: the idea that extraterrestrial invaders interrupted the Starseed Experiment of otherworldly light beings by disassembling the complex DNA network of *Homo sapiens*' celestial origins and scattering them in the dissonance of their electromagnetic nets—resulting in those unconnected bits of "junk" within you.

It is just as unlikely that conventional medicine and biology will arrive at an understanding of how, in scrambling those light-coded filaments, those same E.T. aggressors, the Annunaki lords, deactivated the pineal gland and nullified its primary functions.

With only the double helix of your essential DNA to manage, the ultimately important pineal gland, once ten times its volume, shrank to a size smaller than a pea within your brains and became classified, along with the so-called cerebral "grey matter," as a relevantly insignificant part of the human being's incredible neural and endocrinal systems.

So it has remained, throughout human evolution, until now, as you become fully conscious of your multidimensional nature and your starseeded origins, reconnecting the wires, so to speak, of your cosmic intelligence … identifying what have always been considered superfluous bits and pieces—the "junk"—in your incredibly articulate internal communication networks.

Now that you are integrating the third strand, the pineal gland, great way station for the light of the Cosmos, is expanding—as are you. Know that the retrieval of the third strand of DNA, which calls the pineal gland back to active service, is the giant step for all that will follow, as you become flooded with the brilliance and the beauty of all that you are meant to be.

The primary triangulation, your vibrational "anchor," will hold you together when you move through the Great Vortex and it is that primary triangulation that prepares you for the rebundling and activation of the complete twelve-stranded DNA complex: four times the trinity that is being birthed within many of you now. The cosmometry of that process is so brilliant and simple ... and yet you can easily overlook it because your expectations and an extensive network of misinformation (some intentional, some merely misguided teachings of the well-intended) often cloud your vision of what is occurring now and what lies ahead of you.

Let us walk into the cool green forest of your purest thoughts together—hand in hand, heart in mind—as we merge and unite our energies and thought forms through the dimensions ... now that you are reclaiming your multidimensional awareness, and Ra draws you ever closer to the point of your final passage into the next dimension.

If you feel guided to let us show you the way to activate the third strand of DNA, we can provide it through the crystallization of our thoughts in the printed words below (which you will need to record and play back to guide you into deep meditation). Also available to you is the channeled guidance we have delivered through the instrument in the recording of *The Starseed Awakening.** We ask that you choose the method that feels right for you and recognize the time of your readiness before you proceed.

---

* *The Starseed Awakening*—creative visualizations and guided meditations CD, available through www.sirianrevelations.net

You may prefer to work directly (where possible) or indirectly through the guidance of our instrument, who has been trained and instructed to prepare 144,000 first-wave ascension team members to serve as DNA facilitators, or you may elect to move through the process on your own. You will know which path is right for you.

DNA Activation: Primary Triangulation

Prepare yourself for a deep meditation by lying on the floor, your head pointing north, feet south. You will be facilitated by wearing very loose-fitting clothing, with no restrictions whatsoever upon your body, and eliminating as best as you can all metals from your immediate field.

Create whatever is needed to assure that you are comfortable and uninterrupted, and when you have achieved that peaceful state, lie quietly and begin to breathe deeply and rhythmically, eyes closed, letting the sensate world slowly fall away from you ... slipping into a place of calm and deep relaxation. With every breath, feel yourself becoming more centered and peaceful and the body lighter and lighter ... so light you feel like a feather carried gently in the breeze.

Imagine that you are in an open meadow, filled with the warmth of the Sun and the sweet scent of the trees— where wildflowers abound. You are encircled in the serene splendor of nature, completely at one with all the living beings of your world, feeling your soul lifting higher as it resonates to the music of all-life.

A rainbow appears overhead—painting the sky with the vibrations of your very being. You visualize the crown chakra opening, like the petals of the lotus, as you prepare to accelerate your vibration **forever.**

Breathe deeply, drawing the rainbow refractions of light into the crown, down through the spine, washing down through the chakras, and grounding in the muladhara chakra at the base of your spinal column.

Experience the spectrum of light as your body resonates to the waves that are pouring through you. Feel these energies scintillate within you. Observe how every cell in your body reflects the rainbow, each its own being, each a unit of godliness that defines who you are and what you are capable of becoming ... of creating.

Exhale ... letting go any energies that have clung to you but which no longer serve you. You can ask that they be released into the earth, to be purified and transmuted in the cool of Gaia's wisdom. Breathe them away, releasing yourself from their hold upon you.

Breathe them away, freeing the spirit, body, and mind of their burden.

With the next breath, draw the golden white light of the angelic realms in through the crown, feeling Spirit move through you, trusting that you are guided in this magnificent journey of awakening.

A form appears above the crown center—a golden tetrahedron spinning gently overhead. It is the fundamental geometrical matrix of your evolving DNA—the sacred foundation of your awakening light body.

Take your time ... bring this tetrahedral form into full focus, observing how the brilliance of its light shimmers through you as it quietly spins overhead, reflecting golden white light everywhere around and within you.

Once you have anchored this rotating form clearly in your vision, draw it into the crown and place it directly over the pineal gland, which sits at the epicenter of your head just behind the bridge of your nose. The pineal gland will be perfectly centered within the tetrahedron if you ask that it be so. Feel that golden light bathe this, the lighthouse of your soul, a sense that will be new to you just as much as it will be a sense of **remembering.**

Positioned at the gateway of your emerging consciousness, the golden tetrahedron serves as the matrix from which you will weave the third strand of DNA into your conscious awareness.

Show yourself the double helix formation of your DNA codex, intelligent architect upon which you have constructed your physical being. Imagine a third DNA thread, weaving itself into the double helix, re-creating the form that has embraced the pineal ... creating triangulation within every cell of your body ...

Three, the resolution of duality, is now being imprinted upon the sacred designs taking form within you.

Know that within every cell of your body a new dynamic—your higher vibration—has begun to manifest, and will that it be so forever. State your intention to every part of your being—every organ, every cell, every subatomic particle, and every unit of consciousness that breathes with you—that you intend that the etheric strands of DNA now crystallize within you as is appropriate to your spirit journey.

They are your birthright.

This is a returning...

An arrival and a departure: the multidimensional journey.

And now, before your return to body consciousness, and only when you are ready to do so, fold in the petals of the lotus, blessing the Light Ones who have assisted you here and taking as much time as you need to integrate the new that is being birthed within you. Taking as much time as you need to integrate this experience.

You will return to your body now. Feel your fingers— move your toes—get the blood circulating...

Lie still, taking all the time you need to come completely back to the room, the space in which you find yourself.

Taking all the time you need...

Taking all the time you need...

We have elaborated the importance of the primary triangulation in the previous transmission, and we know that you understand its impact and significance not only for you but also for the whole of humankind. Together with master teachers from the higher realms, we are currently serving you as remote facilitators of the process of third strand reassembly, triangulation, and pineal activation.

This is becoming yours. You are beginning to integrate the DNA strand, and many of you will soon find your way to initiating, with greater focus, the work you came in for—the teaching and healing of those who are preparing for this monumental shift in consciousness.

You will know you have fully integrated the third strand and are resonating at those higher frequencies when you have experienced the light of the heightened pineal gland pouring forward from the third eye centers of your heads, illuminating your flight from the deep jungle ... guiding others, too ... just as the beam of a miner's helmet lights the way out of the coal-dark cavern.

It may be a subtle luminescence at first, or there may be a fiery explosion of energy, but **you will know.** However you process this experience, Dear Ones, you will know when you have successfully integrated the third strand, when primary triangulation has been achieved and anchored, and when the dormant pineal gland has been activated.

At that point, you will have calmed the emotional storms that upset and torment you, feeling more vibrant and radiant, and you will experience a surge in your energy levels and auric fields.

With three strands established, you will have created the cosmometric blueprint upon which the secondary triangulation can be overlaid. Having realized this most significant dynamic, the integration of the triad, the eventual process of full twelve-stranded DNA activation is going to be facilitated by the celestial attunements being received by your home planet and the waves of heightened consciousness passing through every living being that inhabits her.

Again, we ask you to always bear in mind that you are to Gaia as is a cell to your own being, as is a molecule to that cell, and so on, past the boundaries of the material realm, where a thought is to a wave as your Sun is to the Universe. We remind you, light beings of all Creation, never to lose sight of those infinite realities that you have yet to wholly comprehend and envision, in the greatness of the All That Is, That Ever Was, and That Always Will Be.

Secondary Triangulation: The Star Tetrahedron

Secondary triangulation, the activation and synthesis of the fourth, fifth, and sixth strands, will be achieved not as a sequential process, whereby you acquire one strand after another but simultaneously—a perfect triad of light strings resonating as one major chord in the symphony of light playing through you.

Once integrated into the matrix, this exquisite light unit, the higher dimensional reflection of the primary triangulation, will send enormous frequencies coursing through the nuclei of all the cells of your bodies and pulsate (first **through** you and then **from** the nuclear mind) the intricate rhythms and proportions of a complex star tetrahedron, which you are learning is the cosmometric model of the merkaba energy fields that surround you.

Its complex structure represents the unity of the principles of form, purpose, and order with those of space, force, and duration.

The merkaba manifests within every cell of your bodies, reflecting through the human DNA matrix the photonic "memory" of the galactic fields of intelligence coded into your being from the beginning, when *Homo sapiens* touched the Earth, ever so briefly, as fully luminous light-bodied super beings.

When this, the second major phase of your corporeal and spiritual awakening, is realized, your auric fields will extend enormously, merging and exchanging your energies with those of the other in ways you have yet to know and celebrate, however great is the capacity of the expanding human heart and your growing compassion for all the living beings of your world. Your increasing brilliance, which will manifest as a luminous glow that emanates from your crowns, the third eye, the palms of your hands, and the soles of your feet, will illuminate and dramatically alter the environment in which you pass and take shelter.

So will that essence alter realms that you enter solely in etheric form, as pure consciousness—spiritual spectators, Bringers of light. Your gentle radiance will reverberate endlessly through the ethers, the soul of Gaia, through the body of Ra, and across the limitless dimensions of the Cosmos of Soul.

We ask you to consider the microcosmometric expression of those expansive merkaba energy fields, which extend great distances from your physical bodies, defining your "I am" awareness in the etheric realms. You will have an idea, however limited by your current points of reference and observation, of just how powerful the secondary triangulation will be in enhancing your awareness and altering your biological configurations. This occurs at the molecular level, as your mutating DNA acquires new levels of complexity and the wisdom of the Universe springs forward from those golden light strings; it manifests in the "before" of the molecular units—the subatomic particles—spinning into being the new that is constantly being birthed within you; it occurs further yet into the "before" (which is the "beyond," the "after," and the "now"), where Spirit thinks matter into form, and "ahead," where you relinquish the density of those coalesced forms and return to the light.

Secondary triangulation will occur for certain spiritual mas-

ters, assigned ascension team leaders, and active Earth
within a very short time, or, more precisely, at a point on the
time-space continuum to which they are becoming attuned at
this point in their spiritual progression.

They came into this incarnation for this purpose, fully aware
that theirs was to be a lifetime of service, and they are committed to you and to the goddess, Gaia. They have placed the needs
of humankind above their own personal needs and agendas, and
you can sense this selflessness through their work of teaching,
healing, and guiding you into the inner sanctum of your own
divinity.

They are your loving servants, as will be many of you now
preparing as first-wave ascension team members, to assist those
who will follow on the second and so on, until all those who are
intent upon participating in the ascension have come up to the
brilliance. Let their light serve as your lantern, as you pass
through these last initiations—the darkest tunnels of the collective soul journey—through which you are now passing, on your
way to the Dawn.

With six strands of DNA fully integrated, you will be releasing yourselves from some of the most difficult aspects of your
current walk through the illusion. You will alter your body's
patterns of health and well-being, having brought enormous
photonic energies into the molecular matrix.

Virus, invasive bacteria, and thought forms born of disharmony within you cannot withstand such brilliance, and they will
simply have to detach and let go, for they cannot exist at those
frequencies.

That which you have initiated with the release of blocked energies and cling-on thought forms, in the process of activating the third strand, will be exalted—from cell to cell, through the blood, every tissue and organ of the body, and out, into the ethers, radiating wellness and the ecstatic fire of your blessed beings.

At this point, Dear Ones, no dead animal foods will pass through you, for you will be unable to ingest death and suffering: the darkness. You will desire and be capable of digesting only the seed, leaf, and fruit for your nourishment, and these you will find are still abundantly available to you as organic produce—because your societies are demanding that purity ever more as your awareness increases and because more of you are talking to the Earth, asking for assistance, showing your respect and worship.

More of you are becoming devoted caretakers of the soil and the waters of Earth, conscious and vigilant, and you, the ecologists, will be given what you need to hold the resonance. Like the first Atlanteans, you will be even more attuned to the essential energies of the plant foods; you will ask and receive their permission before assimilating their light-bearing essence into your bodies.

Their blessings will then be showered upon you; the fruits of that exchange will be born of the reverence that you hold for the Kingdoms of the Light Bearers.

Others, those trained in breathing for life, will have achieved that level of resonance whereby the unencumbered flow of prana will be all that is required for the body's survival. A very few masters and ascetics have achieved this state at this time; however, far more will be sustained through pranic breathing alone, once the secondary triangulation has manifested in greater numbers of the population.

Theirs is a specific discipline that requires absolute mastery over the physical body, and it is a superb reflection of their will and their ability to exercise mind over matter—but it is not a necessary process for the awakening and transition that will be yours when you reach the stage of secondary triangulation.

It is the birdsong that initiates the flower's bloom, signaling the time of its opening. It is that sweet music and the vibrational keys that move through the ethers, which call the rose from its bed in the circadian rhythms of nature. Trust that you, too, will hear the melody playing to you, and so will you open your multi-colored petals, when the soul calls you to remembrance.

Gaia, the fertile field of the human collective, is always there, setting the rhythm with the beating of her heart. Like a grand maestro, she builds her celestial orchestra by evoking within each of you the pace and inspiration for all that you have trained to bring to the symphony.

You are her notes, the wam vibration; you are her instruments; you are the Music of the Spheres.

So be patient, trusting that what you have seeded and set in motion with the activation of the third strand and your unfailing commitment to goodness, service, and the silenced ego will soon blossom in the new light of Ra. The secondary triad, still the illusive reflection of the primary triangulation, will weave into the matrix when your spirit arrives at that point on the time-space continuum where the resonance board for six-stranded DNA consciousness is activated.

From the perspective of cosmometrical significance, the universal wisdom expressed through the archetypes of number and form, you will realize that the Secret Wisdom—*as above, so below, and as below, so above*—is being imprinted within the nuclear mind of every cell of your bodies as the self-enforcing nature of the interlocking triangulation, Pythagoras's "form of forms," is imprinted upon the waters of your being, crystallizing as six strands of DNA.

This, the crystalline formation that represents, both in its physical and etheric aspects, your interconnectedness to the celestial deities and the Earth Mother, etches the snowflake's exquisite symmetry into every single aspect of your perfecting body, mind, and soul.

Supraluminescence: The Nonagon

You will now be asked to stretch your imaginations (as you have done throughout our teachings) just a bit further, so that you can visualize upon the mind's multidimensional viewing screen that which will be imprinted upon those models of rebundled DNA filaments (those we have described as the "primary" and "secondary" triangulations) with the activation of the third trinity of DNA: the seventh, eighth, and ninth strands.

We are talking here about triangulation "triangulated" within you—the ultimate experience of the essential form, the triad.

This is the exaltation of that form, the superlative ... the Supraluminescence. With the activation of the three trinities, woven into one master cord of light, the expression of each triangulation is taken to its quintessential manifestation within you, giving birth to the triple goddess in every cell ... every aspect of your existence, while you are still earth-bound and preparing for passage.

You are asked to contemplate how the vibrational energies of all numerical archetypes, representative of the cosmometrical proportions and vibrations that comprise not only your universe but also the fundamental nature of the Cosmos of Soul, will be brought into manifestation within you. Nine is the completion and the enclosure of numerical archetypes, and with its vibration, three times trinity, the magnificent library of all cosmometric design will be symbolically registered and imprinted within you.

Like the Egyptians' trinity of trinities, comprised of nine Neteru (archetypes of cosmic order and regulation), so will you— as light bearers of nine cords of cosmic light—come to embody the cosmometric proportions of every vibration throughout Creation.

The Children of the Violet Oversoul have just begun to come in at this level now. Their primary function, as guides and models of your evolutionary species, is to reflect back to you the full light of your ancestral birth, now being reconnected as you master the alchemical formulas of our Elders—recognizing and reclaiming your galactic heritage.

At this highly developed stage of your passage, Dear Ones, you will be so close to passage that you will have stopped thinking about the process itself. Indeed, the aperture of your lens will be so extensive that you will no longer be focused upon yourselves and the immediacy of your lives and personal experiences. We anticipate, judging from our own passing, that you will be so awed by what is transpiring in the Cosmos, so enormously Radiant, that a new sense of identity will pervade all prior consciousness of self.

Confining and detrimental personal relationships, those of the "conditional" nature, will fall away for, like the virus, they, too, cannot cling to you in the light of these immense frequencies.

Limiting emotions simply will not reach resonance with you. Only heart-centered unions will manifest for you at this level of awakening, and that will be of such a vast magnitude that you will reach across the oceans and those "uncharted" seas of the Cosmos with the boundless, infinite love of all existence ... love that pours from you, to you ... through you.

The unfathomable light and universal intelligence that occurs at this level will bring to every aspect of your conscious existence a higher expression and meaning that is so close to pure spirit essence that you begin to "detach," in a sense, from the earthly realm.

At this stage of your wondrous evolutionary passage, you will be absolutely committed to raising Gaia, knowing that the human condition and the myriad life forms of her exquisite being are being vibrationally recorded in the fourth dimension. Bringing her through at the highest vibration that your love and unity can create will set the tenor of the music of man—music that will ring eternal through the dimensions, when you all move through.

And remember ... Gaia, your beautiful Earth, is the communication chakra of your solar system. As she sings, so does the entire body of Ra and the song of the Sun ripples across the galaxies, sounding through the dimensions of the All That Is, That Ever Was, and That Always Will Be.

Four Times Trinity: The Perfected Vortex of Light

At that point on the time-space continuum where Ra **initiates** the final phase of passage and Gaia moves onto the "birthing chair," marked (on your time lines) by the closing of the Mayan calendar, those of you who will be ascending will have reached that level of refinement of "internal cosmometrical relationships" that will trigger the fourth triangulation (the tenth, eleventh, and twelfth strands) into the DNA matrix—achieving four times trinity: the Perfected Vortex of Light.

Being of twelve-stranded DNA consciousness, you will be in perfect synchronicity with every light being of the material realm—those who walk with you, those that have clustered as stellar families to scintillate in the heavens as the twelve archetypal constellations—just as you will have total reconnection and recall of the forgotten seed of your origins.

The galactic portraits of your true ancestry and all that has been lost of the story of humankind will appear before you at the reading of the Akashic Record, and never again will you forget the greatness that brought you to this most magnificent moment of moments. This you will bring forward, for your story is every bit the "future" as it is the "past."

The connections all fit together perfectly—the veil lifts forever and the memory of who you are, *Homo sapiens,* returns at last.

Having achieved light-body presence on Earth, you will have reached that stage of growth and karmic completion—the polishing of the inner crystal—whereby you will no longer need to return to the schools of *samsara.*

At long last, ancient souls, you will bid farewell to the density, the struggle, and the shadow, for the Great Initiation will be over.

You will have passed the tests.

All who have reached full DNA stranding will link consciousness for the magnificent task of breathing Gaia through the birthing process, breathing prana through you and into the body of the Goddess—rhythmically, in absolute synchronicity with the pulsations pouring in from the Sun, as you arrive at the birthing point. Breathing in prana, releasing, breathing in, releasing ... reaching the cataclysmic moment when you have breathed the new into being and emerged at the other side.

Here you will know the One Coded Master; you will now be able to perceive her presence as the Celestial Overseer of Ra's Ascension. She will set the pace of the One Breath, bringing you into perfect resonance with the new of Gaia as your planetary goddess takes that last gasp of density, bursting forward, with the Absolution and purity of the higher realm—as do you.

All Great Masters appear before you, the Angelic Warriors, the Overlighting Ones ... all the Light Ones of the Cosmos will be there to see you through, playing the Music of the Spheres through your instrument: the Soul Collective of the New Dawn.

At long last, we will stand before you and **you will know us,** as you will finally know yourselves. You will hear our voice, realizing that you have heard its whisper in the wind ... all along. You will feel the waves ripple through you as our love races through those golden light strands—the intelligence highways of your souls—into your hearts, into your souls, into the light of your beings.

Godspeed, Dear Ones.

The celebrations are about to begin.

17

Children of the Violet Oversoul

With all we have told you of the shifting vibrations of your complex solar system (and considering your own exquisite perceptions, knowledge, and intuitive sense of what is unfolding in the Universe), it should come as no surprise to you that the explosive energies of the solar deity in ascension and all the reflections and manifestations of that process are being received, registered, and recorded throughout the space that you refer to as the "Milky Way Galaxy"—and out onto the high seas of the universe of matter.

Moreover, those exalted vibrations dance through the higher realms, eternally sounding the keys of innumerable octaves, while playing the dizzying music of the spinning celestial spheres.

All this is pure bliss to heavenly ears.

These celestial reverberations have been reaching countless alien nations, which has everything to do with why you are experiencing such intense extraterrestrial visitation in and around earth orbit, of which we will speak at greater length in short order.

In the meanwhile, do not be too terribly surprised if you look up into the night skies one dreamy evening and happen to observe unusual light formations hovering over the city skyline or see strange-looking airships darting furtively across the dark horizon. Curious, you may check with your local media and civil authorities, only to find that reports of unidentified craft are everywhere abounding—and that the numbers of sightings and close encounters with unexplainable phenomena are increasing almost wildly, with every new day that passes.

By now, you must surely have realized that these previously "unidentifiable" objects (UFOs) are being clearly identified by people the world over! No matter how great the denial of the authorities, you can no longer dismiss the fact that thousands of individuals (many of whom are military, police, commercial air pilots, and astronauts) are experiencing, firsthand, a variety of disks, triangles, and unfamiliar forms flying and hovering over-head. Some (but not all) of these are alien observation craft that have come in to earth sovereignty so that they can sample and evaluate just what is transpiring on your planet.

Your Sun's ecstatic fire is simultaneously pulsing its blazing fury beyond the confines of your three-dimensional territories—into parallel universes and onto the higher realms. This excites those spirit warriors who have moved far beyond the wheel of karma and the physical planes to step down their vibrations in order to reach resonance with the ascending stellar essence: Ra Emerging.

It is, after all, a remarkable cosmic happening, and the whole of the Universe is watching and listening to what is being brought to manifestation: there in your world, the earth kingdom; on and within the neighboring planets, moons, and celestial bits that comprise the body of your solar logos; beyond Ra's immediate sphere of influence, in the whole of the canopy of stars.

Although the majority is still in denial of such fundamental biological probabilities as those posed by the idea that you share this vast Universe with countless other beings, it is time that your contemporary civilization, like so many others who walked before you, realized that you of the Earth are not alone out there in galactic space.

Soon the human race is going to be faced with irrefutable evidence and forced to confront the fact that what you have been told are the "sterile" planets and moons of your complex solar system are actually thriving, bustling worlds. Most are populated with intelligent life forms, myriad animal and insect species and plant kingdoms that are often surprisingly similar to the biological archetypes of your favorite planet. There, too, are dedicated lightworkers, who, like you, are preparing the way of their imminent personal and planetary transformation.

Your entire quadrant of physical space is quite the focus point of light beings who have attuned to your Sun's emissions—those that reside there with you, in the three-dimensional theater of Earth and your solar family, and those of us that co-exist at higher dimensional frequencies.

The waves that permeate our "space" stimulate the spirit warrior curiosity of the Light Forces to explore with the highest of intentions just what monumental occurrences are unfolding in the lower dimensions, from which the deity is emerging, and how those events are playing out for the conscious units that form the bodies of those worlds.

We believe that the desire of an ascended spiritual being to connect with an entire soul collective in transition and that spirit's willingness to come back into the density of its creation are two supreme expressions of universal love and service. We recognize this devotion at every level and juncture, reminding you that there are those of you who have come into the incarnation to stand for humankind and fight for Gaia, and you are of that same intensity and purity of Spirit: warriors all.

Your numbers are increasing dramatically, now that you are remembering who you are and what you have come to do.

Blessed be! We give thanks to the greatness of Spirit: to all who have come before and all who will follow.

Let us forever celebrate the Wisdom and the Way of Supreme Being: the All That Is, That Ever Was, and That Always Will Be.

⁖⁚⁖⁚⁖

Throughout existence, those spirit warriors who have progressed further along the spiral upon which you journey have sometimes retrograded into lower states of consciousness, for however long their service was needed ... flashing the sword of Truth through the ethers and across the plains.

They are there, leading the battles of justice and freedom, on many levels—walking in body amongst the ranks, as an integral part of the soul progression that has gathered at the horizon. They come first in silence, then raising the voice of the collective, dedicating themselves to the rebirthing of the deity and providing aid and guidance to those who, like you, are intent upon serving in that wondrous process. They come to help guide you through the gateway and to seal the celestial parting, for, in the galactic quadrant where your Sun has held resonance until now, only the dwarf star will remain.

Ra's brilliance will be missed.

We are well aware of their impact and significance—for we, too, were pulled from the quagmire of intense polarity and conflict at the time of Sirian ascension. With the help and guidance of so many strong and loving hands and our own free-willed determination, we took command of our inner kingdoms and assisted in the rebirthing of our home planets.

Trust us when we tell you, from a place of humility, that we are aware (to some extent) of what lies ahead of you.

We want you to know that what you bring into the "I am" experience is, to a significant degree, as much ours as it is yours, so it should not surprise you that the Light Forces of the Universe are so involved in your process. As all souls climb higher, all realize that it is our godliness that extends the hand of spiritual solidarity to the others, children of our children, helping the struggling through their paces . . . and being helped through our own.

Ours is the outstretched hand of Prime Creator—the loving support that pulls us all ever upward in the infinity of "moments," one steady stream of light, penetrating the varying layers of darkness, moving us all towards perfection in the godliness of our own creation.

Reach out . . .

Take our hand, that we may guide you through.

There are many expressions of this loving soul presence in the Cosmos . . . so many layers of consciousness permeate the higher realms. Hovering everywhere about you are the Great Archangels, their Angel Warriors, the Ascended Masters, Overlighted Ones, Christed Extraterrestrials, Spirit Warriors, Celestial Deities, Spirit Guides, Essential Spirits, the Bodhisattvas, and countless other light beings ... all in service. All are there to guide souls in progression, which we all are, and all assist when even a single soul jumps off the wheel of karma and passes over the threshold to join us in the Kingdoms of Light.

You can imagine, then, what must be brought forward to prepare the way for the emergence of such a magnificent deity as Ra, with all the combustion and shifting energies that his ascension from three-dimensional consciousness is creating in the Cosmos of Soul ... and with so many souls ascending.

So many souls ...

Reflecting upon that thought, we must admit that it may very well be the case that you cannot yet imagine the significance of Ra's process, nor the undulations that will traverse the cosmic seas when such incredible numbers of beings ascend on one wave, for, like a *tsunami,* it is so vast and so colossal that it is almost unfathomable—even to us, despite our own experience of the Sirius Shift.

We remind you that the primary intention of all the Forces of Light is to illuminate the way of all conscious beings back to Source. The Archangels—Michael, Rafael, Ariel, and Gabriel—oversee the primordial forces of the Universe, balancing the celestial beings and illuminating the heavens. Some light beings are dedicated to specific realms, others to certain species; some work from the higher realms, guiding you ... surrounding you with light; some, such as the Elementals, work within you, through the crystals of your earthly manifestation.

Certain beings are dedicated to you individually—your spirit guides. Others, like the Yzhnüni, who entered at the dawn of the Atlantean civilization, commit to retrograding back into the density of your current realm, to serve entire civilizations of intelligent beings in transition. This is particular to moments such as these, during which such enormous shifts occur that the Warriors of Light feel compelled to fall behind on their steadfast climb, in service to the collective consciousness that resonates to those points on the time-space continuum.

This is the case of the Children of the Violet Oversoul.

We ask you always to remember that, no matter what point we believe we have reached in our social development or spiritual progress, it is essential that we never lose sight of our ultimate responsibility—not only to ourselves as seekers of enlightenment but also to all those who are co-creating the reality—every layer, every shade—right there with us.

As we have told you over and over again ... all is in a state of becoming in the Cosmos of Soul.

Let us now discuss the Children of the Violet Oversoul, incarnating spirit warriors who have made the commitment to enter the earth arena to help see you through the Desert Days of your transcendence—from the density of your tumultuous world into the next dimension.

We wish to identify who they are and what is their role on Earth, so that we may eliminate some of your confusion in their regard, for there are all levels of highly aware souls coming in at this time.

There are the psychic children, the Indigos, walk-ins, and yes, even hybrid extraterrestrials, with enormous capacities, walking amongst you now. Not all of these talented and gifted new-comers to the Earth realm are necessarily the dedicated spirit warriors of earth ascension, however, so be aware of just what it is you are celebrating when you speak of the "gifted" children.

The Violet Oversoul is a collective of highly evolved spirit warriors who vibrate at the high end of the spectrum of light that permeates the physical realm.

They travel on the violet ray.

Light-bodied beings who have long ago completed their karmic commitments in the training schools of the material realms, they have volunteered to sacrifice their own evolutionary achievements and retrograde back in at the lower end of the spectrum—there in the physical light of Ra—in dedicated serv-ice to the mind, body, and spirit of Gaia.

Other warrior teams are entering in order to assist the sister deities of Gaia, planets of your solar system that will be ascend-ing along with you, directed by the One Coded Master ... who is creating the appropriate links and harmonies and setting the tempo that will move you all through in perfectly harmonious overtones and divine synchronicity.

Know that the Violet Oversoul is only now entering the earth space; just a moment has passed since these light beings have begun to come through to serve as ascension models for those of you who can recognize them. Their assignment is to assist in disintegrating the grid and to shine the light for the ascension teams, who are calling you all to duty for the human race, the animals, and the elements of the Earth. They have come to illu-minate the threshold through which you soon will pass—recep-tive, awake, united.

The Children of the Violet Oversoul are coming in with nine strands of DNA—the Supraluminescence—light abounding. Their presence will be key to your anchoring of the triangulated triad, when you reach the point where you have integrated the nine strands of the nonagon.

Their primary points of entry, or birth stations, correspond to twelve strategic locations on the planet, an icosahedral configuration, re-creating the cosmometry of the crystallized twelve-stranded DNA structures of *Homo sapiens,* Gaia's cellular units. At these nevralgic nexus points of the Earth, the electromagnetic grid is at its weakest, not surprisingly, since the sacred geometry of those vortices creates its own powerful vibratory fields. This is essential to the Oversoul's capacity to deflect the grid and hold full nine-stranded awareness for the time the Children have chosen to walk amongst you in light body.

The renewed frequencies emanating from the activated sacred sites of these birth points will surround and penetrate the planetary body—emitting waves of light that will extend to the four corners of the Earth and intersect at the epicenter of the inner world of Agharta, the world you know as Shambhala.

Since the days of ancient Atlantis, when your great ancestors found their way to safety in Earth's inner core, the safeguarding of the Gaian spirit has been directed from that inner place— home of the Aghartan leadership, the heart center of the goddess. Over the ages, they have secretly received and trained the descendants of the Atlantean White Brother-Sisterhood, who have reincarnated on various pages of the history books but most often imprinted the unwritten human story.

Deep within this sanctuary of the inner Earth, the High Priests and Lamas of countless eras have been given the keys to the treasury of Aghartan knowledge, but they were to keep them hidden from view—in safekeeping—until this time, when all is to be revealed. They are every bit as integral to this divine adventure as are you, residents of Earth's outer world.

Although access to the Land of Agharta remains a secret to all but the anointed, your rising awareness is beginning to reach into the inner chamber and find resonance there. You are being touched by the Ascended Masters who regularly visit the magical land, bringing back to the outer spheres the light of the inner realm. More of you have begun to journey in astral body through the labyrinth that will lead you to the hallowed hallways of Agharta. Soon, now, the doorways of the city will be opened.

Always remember that from your current sense of "direction," where "above" is of the heavens and "below" is in some nebulous place in the soils of Gaia—you often forget that the "within" of your heavenly mother is the heart, the pulse, and the Center of her existence.

The sacred heart of Gaia is found in Agharta.

There, adorning the High Altar, the Holy of Holies, sit the Ark and the Covenant.

⁂

Despite the existing electromagnetic grid and the bombardment of Extremely Low Frequency waves of the HAARP transmitters, the Children of the Violet Oversoul have been capable of stepping down their frequencies and crystallizing their essence in the slowed fields of Earth's "contained" energies by selecting specific locations of emergence on the planet where the imposed grid is its weakest ... or breaking down completely.

They entered in the millennium year 2000 and are still in the child stage by your biological measures ... yet they are as ancient as time itself.

They chose to go through the process of birth in its entirety, fully aware of every phase of their embryonic development, in order to recall every detail of the experience of crystallizing from spirit into form—just as all souls transiting Earth—old and new—have done, but have forgotten.

Their process required that they participate, fully awake, in the explosive union of paternal and maternal consciousness—the impregnation of the ova—and that they illuminated those conjoining energies with the purifying light of the violet ray—burning away all karmic imprints of the father and mother and clearing the way for the fertile fields in which to seed.

At that moment of crystallization of form, the Violet Oversoul imprinted the triangulated triad of light filaments into the matrix of the ascending starseeded human race. The fetal environment, the sacred womb, was of the Luminescence; the mothers radiated the brilliance.

In those nine months of gestation, nine luminous strands of DNA were imprinted within every cell of their crystallizing light bodies and all was in a state of exaltation at the time of their emergence—their fully conscious birth into the restrictive bands of earth reality.

You will recognize significant patterns of sacred geometry unfolding with their arrival: four times trinity reflected around the globe.

Twelve Children of the Violet Oversoul have been born in this way in twelve locations: the 144,000-petaled lotus of the goddess heart has opened. They will reach the solar age of twelve years when the final stage of the ascension has been initiated, in the twelfth month of the earth year 2012 (twenty twelve), when the eleven-year cycle of solar peak, which initiates just prior to the onset of the calendar 2012, enters its twelfth year—around the closing of the twelfth month of 2012.

The Twelve Tribes will have reconvened around the Aghartan leadership—there at the Center, the thirteenth, where all twelvefold order convenes. The circle of twelve crystal skulls will be reunited, bringing the central Master Skull to crystallize again upon the Earth.

The Skull Committee will have been activated; the pineal within every member of the ascension team will have reached full illumination.

The Children of the Violet Oversoul will achieve twelve-stranded DNA consciousness at that time, and the scintillations of their luminescence will ignite the strands within you.

The One Coded Master will have completed the master blueprint.

All will be synthesized for your passage through the great vortex of Ra's ascending body, mind, and spirit.

18

Contact

We are well aware of the difficulties you face when you attempt to bring the excitement of what you have gleaned from our indirect communications, your otherworldly visions, and your multidimensional journeys to the greater body of your fellow earth residents. Entrained, as most of the race currently is, to the lower vibrations, frozen in fear or dulled by the narcotics that proliferate at all levels of your contemporary societies, they simply cannot hear your message of hope and bright tomorrows—but that, too, is going to change in the very near moment of revelation—when Truth will lift the veils.

To all but a very distinct minority of determined and courageous seekers, thoughts of extradimensional beings speaking to the people of Earth through select channels such as ours are utterly ridiculous, and you are damned as the gullible and foolish if you dare attempt bringing your experience of our teachings (and those of others you deem worthy of your trust and acceptance) to the open public.

To speak of those vibrational shifts that occur from the mere reading of these words, as so many of you have reported to us and to others, is to jeopardize one's credibility, to invite condemnation ... to risk even retaliation from those who do not want you to go about spreading light there, where they have so painstakingly painted the halls of history in darkness and deceit.

We know. We have stood at Trydjya's side throughout, observing her process, pointing the way around those hurdles that have not yet been surmounted and finding new avenues where our message can be heard and carried to the awaiting ... lightworkers such as you. We are delighted that you were paying attention when the book "fell off the shelf," reconnecting us ... and we are grateful that you are showing so many others to that same library.

Now, however, is the time for the whole of humankind to read between the lines of all that has been etched into the community ledgers.

Let there be no more secrets, no more lies.

⁖⁘⁘⁖

Meanwhile, the power elite continue to bombard the collective unconscious with fearful and utterly frightening images of alien archetypes (and plenty do they know of dark beings, near and far!) in order to hold your wandering minds at bay. Rather than having you roam the Universe, fascinated by the glorious potential of your membership in the Galactic Federation of Worlds, they much prefer you lock your vivid imaginations into the terrifying possibilities of an alien "invasion" of body-snatching creatures, who wish to strip you of your sovereignty and control your bodies, minds, and souls.

How "curiously" ironic that they should see alien activity on Earth in that way, isn't it?

The theater of operations through which they inculcate in the human psyche the lies and misinformation that have allowed them, for countless decades, to hold their knowledge of extra-terrestrial life secret, is played to the global audience through an extensive media campaign, staged abduction rituals, planned night maneuvers of their own alien-designed space craft, and ongoing subliminal messages. Even there, in your own circles of alternative thinkers, deliberate misinformation and false gurus fill you with the dread and fear of just what alien forces will do with you once they land on the White House lawn, climb onto the rooftop of the Kremlin, and slither, cold and silent, into your living rooms.

Then again, if you are one who is prone to such imaginings, it may be opportune that you also consider with what trepidation alien travelers, astronauts of your same galactic meridians, might enter Earth's inhospitable inner orbit, a place filled with threatening devices of every measure and intensity. If they are determined enough to ignore those gigantic **DO NOT ENTER** signs, the frequency bands that your leaders have placed menacingly around your perimeters, they will still have to confront the militarized zones at the surface.

What kind of welcoming committees do you suppose will be there to greet them, if they come in the full light of day?

We trust you realize that we are certainly not going to contradict ourselves by painting a rose-tinted picture, whereby we deny that troublesome entities are being drawn into your space, filling you with reassuring platitudes of an unrealistic scenario. Nor can we validate that growing cult, whose message is that "good" aliens are soon to swoop down with their mother ships on a mission to save you from the evils of your reality, plucking you out of your neighborhoods and whisking you off to new worlds. We are always wary of any "solution" that strips you of your power to create your own realities from an infinite range of experiences and possibilities that are always available to you, as free-willed beings of the Cosmos.

Our intention is that the information of extraterrestrial presence amongst you become public domain, yes, and that there be no fear amongst you. You are the ones who will take the information to experience and interact with those forms when contact is finally made. You must have a clear vision of what this will mean to you as individuals, as representatives of the global society, and for many of you who have already taken the giant leap of awakening to service, as first-wave ascension team members.

You all will have a part in determining the outcome of those first meetings. Will the drums be beating, as they are almost everywhere on Earth, or will your call to celebration rise above the din of your war machinery?

Were it left to the power elite, all extraterrestrial visitors would be deemed the ultimate enemies, harbingers of the final confrontation—the new "terrorists." All alien communication would be "intercepted," and what they would portray to as contact would be manipulated messages of the darkest of dark intentions.

You cannot let that happen, or shall we say that you very well could, but you will not.

Neither will we.

Neither will those who will come.

If only you will raise the joyful voice of your humanity and guide the ships in on the welcoming waves of love and celebration, all threat to your civilization, real or invented, will be aborted.

We do not deny that the material realm is one of varying intensities of polar contrast, where dark and light beings of every imaginable configuration choreograph the duel of opposition—this you know to be true. We have previously confirmed to you that the Government has indeed sold you out for the acquisition of tremendously powerful technologies—those that are now emerging as cutting-edge military weaponry and mind-control devices.

In exchange, their E.T. allies, operating in the earth zone for decades, have been allowed to perform experiments into human and animal biology, forcibly taking specimens from unwilling abductees for their seed and the potential of their latent DNA composition; many of those incidents, we confirm, have been conducted by the Zeta Reticulans, who are presently working alongside of the Secret Government.

Contracts do exist between them ... and you, the human race, were written into the terms of agreement!

Other abduction encounters, in which human victims are heavily drugged and forced to play out the terrifying scenes of alien manipulation, have been conducted by government operatives themselves. Indeed, the majority of all abduction encounters is part of a carefully planned campaign of the Secret Government, which wishes to raise the pitch of your terror to such a peak that you will be literally scared out of your rational minds when the first ships make open contact with the massive earth population.

If you give due consideration to their predicament, you will understand far more about why the Government obstinately continues to conceal its secret knowledge of alien intervention and communication with Earth. Knowing what you do of the reptilian "agenda"—the Annunaki's plan to use the lowered frequencies of your planet to pull Nebiru back from the dark winter of its journey in time for the ascension—you must give due consideration to just what open contact will mean to their ill-fated plan, which holds Earth captive to harvest her energies.

Heightened vibrations of evolved species entering into Earth's fields at this crucial moment, when they are desperately attempting to link Gaia to the base frequencies of Nebiru, will destroy any chance of achieving the "long-shot" goal.

Why, you ask yourselves, is the mass mind of man still stalking about in the jungles, rapaciously killing or being killed in the wilds of dark mind—when you are about to reach the highest peaks of the human journey?

It is because you have been entrained to feed of blood and violence and enslaved to fuel the dark intention, lowering the vibration of Earth ... so that you can reach resonance with the lost planet before it is too late for Nebiru to return.

To understand why your leaders take you to such dark places, you must always remember that the underlying reason why they create so much dissidence and chaos in your world, attempting to destroy the exalted harmonies of the goddess in flight, is, to the Annunaki, a "necessary evil."

⁘⁙⁘

Consider what will occur when extraterrestrial cosmonauts land their ships on earth soil and finally appear—to address the human nation. Imagine it, not as the terrifying *Independence Day* invasion portrayed in the fear film but as the arrival of heretofore "nonexistent" life from outer space—the ultimate new paradigm for your society to cope with and make "human" from that point forward.

Imagine the enormity of such discovery—the limitlessness of its potential significance and the flight of your collective soul, no longer the orphan circumstance of a lifeless universe.

Will not the lives of every living being on Earth be changed forever? Will not all existing power structures be crushed in the wave of human outreach? Examine the possibilities one step at a time, and you will have climbed up the stairway and onto higher ground in your understanding of the establishment's denial.

The moment an alien fleet arrives openly within Earth boundaries, a first natural reaction (considering the negative and fear-evoking propaganda that has forever permeated your consciousness) will be one of total panic. No government will ever be able to convince you (nor will it try) that it has the wherewithal to deal with such an eventuality. Neither will your leaders pretend to protect you from the designs of the "invading," whom they have forever portrayed as the unstoppable forces of hell.

Your first encounter, at the global level, will most likely be one of total chaotic recoil.

Once you have coped with the first shocking images of aliens amongst you, all current control systems will collapse entirely. Wall Street will crash, military options will fail (for if they've arrived, nothing, not even the Star Wars System or the electromagnetic grids, will have been able to stop them), and your already teetering globalized economic society will crumble and fall. All social experience, as you know it, will come to a screeching halt, as you gather around your televisions, awaiting the "doomsday message" of the invaders.

Until the intent of those visitors has been made manifest through their behavior, and until the messages of the galactic newcomers have clarified the situation at hand, not much more than gasps and shudders will blow across the icy fields of those frozen human emotions.

Life as it was before that moment—life as you are living it right now—will never be the same again. At that point in your passing, whereby the entire world population is irrefutably confronted with aliens amongst you, the wars for territory, religion, and race that now define your crises will end **abruptly.** They will simply pale before the spectacle of life from beyond. The loveless eyes of hatred that peer from behind your current fences will all be lifted upward, to gaze upon the boundless fields of the Cosmos.

The Power will have no control over you from that moment on—and this they know all too well.

And so, do not fear contact, for it is just what is needed now—that "miracle" something that will cause a global tidal wave of consciousness to wash across your shores. Alien contact is going to be an event of such magnitude in human affairs that the collective will be shaken from its reptilian trance in time to look up from the blood that has been plated as its food ... to the whirring and stir of what moves overhead.

The Councils of many alien nations have convened and are

moving in, despite the barriers being fortified in earth space. The governments simply cannot prevent you from receiving open contact with representatives of pioneering extraterrestrial civilizations, no matter how they intensify the smoke screen.

Contact is imminent.

You know it is—you realize that the Secret Government cannot keep the evidence from you any longer. You know that the sightings are proliferating everywhere around the world and that even the mainstream media, however silenced to truth, can no longer avoid the unavoidable. People everywhere on Earth have begun to take notice of new lights in the heavens—lights that dance, lights that move about, lights that illuminate the undeniable fact that humankind's isolation is coming to a most exciting end.

Despite the Power's desperate efforts (for desperate they are indeed) to conceal all they know of the alien life that thrives beyond and within your parameters, there is simply no way to prevent your discovery of the hidden domains. Contact is soon to be made with the people of Planet Earth—in your lifetimes. You are all going to experience this, no matter where you stand on the question of human evolution and the coming earth changes.

The Power knows this, for they have been given a deadline in which to announce the news of alien presence in your realm, after which those who intend to stand before you **will.** That deadline, Dear Ones, has just about expired ... and yet they remain silent.

It is quite apparent that they do not intend to honor that commitment because they will then have to come clean on the alien secret. Their vulnerability will seep through their disguises, exposing their scaly underbellies, and they will lose their grip the moment the society—all six billion individual units—understands that the reality they have imposed has been shattered.

The vibrations of the entire human race will raise the nets, and your slavery will be over.

Nebiru will be lost forever—the Annunaki dream will die.

Why have you not been told the truth about extraterrestrial life? We believe it is as clearly evident to you as it is to all who watch over you.

Those dark aliens, who for so long have imposed their rule upon the human race, willed it so. They stripped you of your galactic heritage at your inception, and they have hidden all record of the true nature of the Universe from you, throughout earth time, until now.

That has been the greatest secret of all.

Epilogue

Throughout the volume of words that we have made crystalline for you through these works, *The Sirian Revelations,* we have spoken to you of the infinite layers and dimensions of reality that exist, together, as the All That Is: beings of light and love, forces of darkness and misguided energies, realms of unimaginable brilliance, and others of the density and slowed vibration. We have evoked within you a great many emotions to be faced and dealt with ... and more to be celebrated and exalted. We have shared with you our perspective upon aspects of being that you are experiencing now and what lies just ahead of you.

It is a glorious time for humanity—you will see, if you are still blinded by the dark illusion. Despite the despair and confusion of your immediate world, it is a glorious time for you to be alive.

Ours has been a magnificent ride upon the ethers of your ever-increasing emanations of love and universality, where we have met through the pages of these works and we have been touched, so deeply, by the souls of each and the other.

Blessed be.

Children of beauty and light, you are forever in our hearts.

If only you could see what we see when we look upon your bold, shining faces—mirrors of your innocence and wisdom—and feel your hope coursing through us.

How we wish you could know with certainty that what you dream for the future is the reality, and that what appears to be so terrifyingly real to you now is only a dream of the collective unconscious.

As you ponder the possibilities of what is about to occur for those of you who are determined to ascend to new heights and lighter realms, it is your human nature to fret over the manifestations of such enormous changes. You have yet to override your feelings of worry and concern over the plight of those who will not pass through the vortex at the time of Ra's calling, for no matter what you embrace as your understanding of free-will decisions and the soul's determination before entering, it is contrary to your love of beauty and light to think that any form of life must suffer.

It is still difficult for you to understand that a soul would choose suffering as part of the process it must experience of its own—but you are learning that such is the way of Spirit.

You can light the way for the others, with all the force of your brilliance, and hope that the lost will reach you.

You can help the wounded back to their feet, you can heal the sick, care for the tired, feed the poor ... but in the end, Dear Ones, you must honor the soul decisions of each and of the many.

It may be difficult for you to always stand in your truth, and leave others stand in theirs, for you must let go of so many things. People may become threatened—they may challenge you or move away altogether. We know what you must confront in the world of illusion in order to honor Spirit. Despite your commitment to the light and your understanding of all that has been elucidated in these times of your great awakening, for as long as you are still fighting your way through the storm, clutching your coats as the winds whip about you, it can be overwhelmingly difficult, at times, to stand tall and unwavering—committed to the forward momentum, where love and respect for all beings prevail.

But you do stand for truth, Dear Ones ... your arms reaching out to the heavens above, you stand majestic—as tall as the great oak tree.

We know the obstacles that are placed in your path when you refuse to follow the road that was laid out for you, never straying, never imagining the meadow, never charting your own course ... never daring to be one, to be all, to be free. The obstruction is immense and often appears insurmountable, but you do know, deep within you, that it is nothing more than fear and a resistance to change.

You have it in your Karma Files, which you brought through with you when you decided to come into this earth adventure, that blowing down the establishment walls would be a Herculean task ... but that fall they would indeed.

It would have been easier by far to simply follow the herd, corralled into the fences and confines set for you by the false masters.

Easier, perhaps. But what, then, of the music and the light?

You, the awakeners, came to sing the dawn into being.

Children, we call you all to service.

Breathe deeply, drawing all the love of existence into your hearts ... exhale, letting go of any residual fear that may still lurk within—letting it go forever. And with the next magnificent breath, fill your souls with the knowledge that you are **sovereign beings,** the Guardians of Gaia:

> ... *mighty as her highest mountains*
> *steady as her tallest trees*
> *infinite as her greatest oceans and*
> ***free***
> *as the wind upon her waters.*

Index

About the Channel

A native of the San Francisco Bay Area, Patricia Cori has been immersed in the New Age Movement since its inception there in the early 1970s. She has utilized her clairvoyant abilities in healing and support work throughout her life, which has been dedicated in great part to the study of mysticism and philosophy, ancient civilizations, metaphysical healing, spirituality, and extraterrestrial life.

A world teacher, Patricia is helping many realize their natural healing abilities, release the blockages of unresolved emotions and limitation, attuning to the higher vibrations of our ascending celestial realm. She is currently actively preparing the first-wave ascension teams in the healing and activation of the DNA, so that they can, in turn, facilitate the process in others.

Patricia has lived in Italy since she immigrated to Rome in 1983, knowing that she had to take part in a mission ... as she was instructed by her guides that she would have to help "burn a hole in the lead dome ..." She is a prominent figure in the New Age Movement, well-known on the lecture circuit, offering courses, seminars, and workshops internationally, which reflect her conscious awareness of the Higher Knowledge and the empowering guidance of the light beings working through her.

She has been actively channeling the Speakers of the Sirian High Council since her first visitation to the crop circles in 1996, and continues to lecture and transcribe their messages for all those who seek the wisdom.

Be sure to read her first two books: *The Cosmos of Soul: A Wake-Up Call for Humanity* and *Atlantis Rising: The Struggle of Darkness and Light.* To learn more about her lectures, workshops, and the DNA Facilitators' program, contact Patricia at:

patcori@tiscalinet.it
www.sirianrevelations.net

About the DNA Activation Programs

Patricia Cori offers personal training in DNA activation and certification programs for DNA Facilitators, as directed by the healing teams of the Sirian High Council, in various locations around the world. These are:

Ascension Training Level I
DNA Activation

The process of awakening the light body begins with the healing and release of blocked emotions and thoughts manifest as illness within the physical body, and the reintegration of the fragments of your being that have been left behind along your journey. As you cannot move forward without them, the opening segment of the course will be dedicated to calling them home to you—a most essential aspect of our preparation for ascension.

This two-day intensive course facilitated by Sirian Light Beings focuses on opening the energy byways, drawing from the multidimensional self the innate abilities that will accelerate your preparation for ascension. Guided by Light Beings from many dimensions, you will be shown the way to the new horizons upon the path of your spiritual and emotional experience—preparing the way for the activation of the third strand of DNA and the awakening of the light body.

Activation of the new crystalline matrix that is forming in your evolving being (the integration of the third strand of DNA) creates triangulation within the consciousness of every cell of your physical body—the trinity of divine awareness.

The entire energy body, the chakras and their corresponding glandular systems (particularly the pineal gland), the *ida* and *pingala* energy byways, the auric body—every aspect of existence in the world of matter is about to change, and as one of the awakening, you are eager to accelerate that process.

Those of you who have come in to serve as guides and healers in the process of Gaia's evolution are called to Initiation: the activation of the third strand, chakric clearing, cellular regeneration, resonance with the higher frequencies, and connection with the Galactic Family of Light Beings.

This intensive is intended (but not limited) to those who are ready to take the leap as the first of a two-part training: those who intend to take the Level II DNA Facilitators' Training, during which participants will adjust to the newly attained frequencies and develop specific techniques and procedures to assist others in healing and activating the DNA. They will learn to construct the cosmometric cellular geometries and raise the vibratory frequencies that will prepare the way for activation of the fourth, fifth, and sixth strands, triggering pineal illumination and strengthening their link with the higher beings who are serving in the process.

As we draw upon the patterns of all cosmic consciousness, we will also ground ourselves to Gaia, for this is our celestial home—as it will be for those who choose to ascend into the next dimension, the New Frontier. We do this in absolute integrity, honesty, and conviction—for we are past the time when we can distract ourselves with imaginings, posturing, and spiritual rhetoric. We must clear away the distractions and be prepared to walk in the light of Absolute Truth—at peace in our souls as we climb the spiral of Return.

Ascension Training Level II
DNA Facilitators Program

At the inner level, Level II participants build upon the ongoing process of anchoring the third strand, laying further ground for the assimilation of the second triangulation: the fourth, fifth, and sixth strands, with the opening of the Golden Heart and the accelerated Pineal Gland.

At the community level, where our focus is upon bringing the light and wisdom of the Overlighting Ones to each other, the intensive workshop helps develop a more profound awareness and ability in:

- The work of sound and its healing global and planetary properties
- DNA healing
- Vibrational alteration of individual and environment
- Attunement to galactic grids
- The proper use of channeling for planetary and universal perspectives

At this crucial time of individual and planetary transmutation, students are guided as to the implementation of the service they have chosen to bring to the whole, and the work of serving as first-wave ascension team members in their tribes and communities.

The workshop includes deep meditation work and group toning guided by the Council, training and practice in DNA reading, and instruction for the practical matters of serving as a DNA Facilitator: cellular regeneration, the elemental energies, the properties of conscious water, star linking, and opening the channels of extra-dimensional communication.

Both workshops are also offered in conjunction with Patricia's spirit journeys of initiation at the sacred sites of the world's power points.

> *For additional information about the exciting*
> *SoulQuest™ Journeys & DNA Facilitators' programs*
> *with Patricia Cori,*
> *Please consult her website:*
> *www.sirianrevelations.net*